South-Western

WORDPERFECT® 6.0 DOS

QUICK COURSE

Mary Alice Eisch
OFFICE OCCUPATIONS INSTRUCTOR
FOX VALLEY TECHNICAL COLLEGE
APPLETON, WISCONSIN

SOUTH-WESTERN PUBLISHING CO.

Copyright © 1995
by SOUTH-WESTERN PUBLISHING CO.
Cincinnati, Ohio

ALL RIGHTS RESERVED

The text of this publication, or any part thereof, may not be reproduced or transmitted in any form or by any means, electronic or mechanical, including photocopying, recording, storage in an information retrieval system, or otherwise, without the prior written permission of the publisher.

ISBN: 0-538-63409-X

2 3 4 5 6 H 99 98 97 96

Printed in the United States of America

Editor-In-Chief: *Robert E. First*
Acquisitions Editor: *Janie F. Schwark*
Senior Production Editor: *Mary Todd*
Designer: *Nicola M. Jones*
Consulting Editor: *Judith Voiers*
Cover Photo: *Majory Dressler*

WordPerfect is a registered trademark of WordPerfect Corporation. IBM is a registered trademark of International Business Machines Corporation. South-Western Publishing Co. disclaims any affiliation, association, connection with, sponsorship, or endorsement by their respective owners.

I(T)P
International Thomson Publishing

South-Western Publishing Co. is an ITP company. The ITP trademark is used under license.

Preface

WordPerfect® 6.0 DOS: Quick Course is designed to be a self-teaching guide for users of WordPerfect on IBM® or IBM-compatible equipment. It is written for the lay person in language that is appropriate for high school and adult students. While the text may be used in classrooms, it is also a good resource for secretaries and managers learning WordPerfect in the home or office.

LESSON FEATURES

In addition to the hands-on exercises used to reinforce learning, each lesson contains the following:

- learning objectives
- estimated time for completion
- an explanation of the features and their uses
- a step-by-step guide for using the feature
- written activities to reinforce understanding
- a reference question to acquaint the learner with the WordPerfect documentation

Review exercises are strategically placed to give the learner a break from new material and reinforce previously learned skills.

6.1 UPDATE

Bound into the back of the text is a WordPerfect 6.1 for DOS update containing the following features:

- references to pages in the text where versions 6.0 and 6.1 differ
- explanatory material introducing new features
- exercises to aid in learning the new features

The update is separated from the rest of the text so the text can be used conveniently by either 6.0 or 6.1 students.

STUDENT HELPS

A Study Guide, including lesson titles, estimated completion times, and space to check off completed work, is located on page vii. The Command Reference section that lists WordPerfect features and the keystrokes and menu choices for those features is in the back of the book.

Also available is a template disk containing many of the documents in the hands-on exercises. While the actual keying of the exercise greatly enhances learning, the use of the prerecorded documents may serve to speed up learning.

▶ MANUAL

The *Manual* contains the following:

- teaching suggestions for each lesson
- solutions for the end-of-lesson activities
- solutions illustrating the hands-on exercises
- three production tests with solutions

▶ MESSAGE TO THE LEARNER

It's time to learn to use WordPerfect! You probably already know this, but WordPerfect is a word processing program that can help you create great-looking documents quickly and easily. Not only is it easy to use, it is easy to learn.

This book is based on the assumption that you already know how to use your computer. You might also be familiar with another word processing program. For that reason, most of the explanations about the basics of creating documents have been eliminated, leaving only the instructions for the learning.

In some cases you will encounter an explanation about why WordPerfect works the way it does so that you can better understand the program. Make an effort to think like the program. By doing so, you will be preparing yourself for learning to use features that are not taught in this book–when you will be on your own.

This book also assumes your WordPerfect program has already been installed and is ready to use. In fact, it begins with the working screen already showing. If there is no one to help you get the program started, turn to Appendix A where the various hardware configurations and some basic information about the WordPerfect software are discussed. Installation and start-up instructions are also included, along with instructions for changing drive defaults and changing setups to make your WordPerfect program best fit your situation. Appendix B introduces the use of the mouse, in case you are a new mouse user.

Sit back, relax, and get ready to learn WordPerfect.

Mary Alice Eisch
Appleton, Wisconsin

Contents

Study Guide vii

Lesson 1 **Starting and Exiting WordPerfect** 1

The WordPerfect Screen; Keying Text; Checking the Drive; Saving Text; Opening a Document; Resaving a Document

Lesson 2 **Correcting Text** 9

Moving the Cursor; Adding to a Document; Correcting and Deleting Text; Inserting Text; Paginating Text; Review Exercises

Lesson 3 **File Management** 19

Printing from the Working Screen; Printing from the File Manager; File Management

Lesson 4 **Formatting Text** 25

Character and Word Formatting; WordPerfect Character Sets; Dash Characters and Hard Spaces; Formatting Paragraphs; Indent, Left/Right Indent; Reveal Codes; Review Exercises

Lesson 5 **Changing Formats** 39

Changing Your Mind; Setting Tabs; Setting Margins; Line Spacing; Justification; Changing Defaults; Review Exercise

Lesson 6 **Editing Text** 49

Blocking Text; Formatting Blocked Text; Deleting Blocked Text; Copying and Moving Blocked Text; Moving a Column; Printing and Saving Blocks; Search and Replace

Lesson 7 **Writing Tools** 61

The Speller; The Thesaurus; Grammatik; Hyphenation

Lesson 8 **Miscellaneous Tools** 67

Viewing Documents; The Ribbon; The Button Bar; Bookmarks

Lesson 9 **WordPerfect Tables** 77

Terminology; Create a Table; Edit and Format a Table; Miscellaneous Table Features

Lesson 10 **Merge** 87

Merge Terminology; Creating a Form File; Creating a Data File; Merging the Files; Data Files with Named Fields; Table Data Files; Keyboard Merge

Lesson 11 **Handling Correspondence** 101

Single Envelopes; Merged Envelopes; Labels; Sort; Select; Review Exercises

Lesson 12 **Multiple-Page Documents** 115

Headers and Footers; Page Numbering; Suppress; Footnotes and Endnotes; Page End Control; Other Features; Review Exercise

Lesson 13 **Using Macros**................................... 127

Creating and Playing a Macro; Macro Information; Chained and Nested Macros; Macro Lists

Lesson 14 **WordPerfect Columns and Outlines** 133

Newspaper Columns; Parallel Columns; Outlining; Editing Outlines

Lesson 15 **WordPerfect Graphics**..................... 143

Graphics Boxes; Create a Graphics Box; Text in Boxes; Graphics Lines; Borders; Equations; Miscellaneous Graphics

Appendix A **Hardware and Software**................. 157

Hardware; Installation; Printers; Starting WordPerfect; Changing Drives and Directories; Changing Defaults

Appendix B **Using a Mouse**............................... 163

Hand Position; Clicking; Menus; Blocking Text

Command Reference... 165
Index 173
WordPerfect 6.1 for DOS Update U1
WordPerfect 6.1 for DOS Special Features U3

Study Guide

Name _____

Lesson	Score	Date Completed	Instructor
LESSON 1 Starting and Exiting WordPerfect — 1/4 HOUR			
LESSON 2 Correcting Text — 1/4 HOUR			
LESSON 3 File Management — 1/4 HOUR			
LESSON 4 Formatting Text — 1 1/2 HOURS			
LESSON 5 Changing Formats — 1 HOUR			
LESSON 6 Editing Text — 1 HOUR			
PRODUCTION TEST 1			
LESSON 7 Writing Tools — 1/2 HOUR			
LESSON 8 Miscellaneous Tools — 1 HOUR			
LESSON 9 WordPerfect Tables — 2 HOURS			
LESSON 10 Merge — 1 1/2 HOURS			
LESSON 11 Handling Correspondence — 1 1/2 HOURS			
PRODUCTION TEST 2			

Name

Lesson		Score	Date Completed	Instructor
LESSON 12 Multiple-Page Documents	½ HOUR			
LESSON 13 Using Macros	½ HOUR			
LESSON 14 WordPerfect Columns and Outlines	¾ HOUR			
LESSON 15 WordPerfect Graphics	½ HOUR			
PRODUCTION TEST 3				

LESSON 1

Starting and Exiting WordPerfect

OBJECTIVES

Upon completion of this lesson, you will be able to:

1. Discuss the WordPerfect working screen.
2. Discuss the three WordPerfect 6.0 screen modes.
3. Create a simple document using default settings.
4. Name and save a document and exit from WordPerfect.

Estimated Time: 1/2 hour

   WordPerfect is a powerful program to be used for the creation of documents of all kinds. You can prepare letters, reports, newsletters, invoices, memos, and just about any other kind of document you can imagine using this tool. As with other tools, you must learn enough about it so you can use it efficiently. All of the advanced hardware and software in the world isn't much good to you if it takes you longer to prepare the document than it did with the old-fashioned tools.

   In this lesson you will learn about the WordPerfect 6.0 for DOS interface. What does the working screen look like? How should you view your document as you work with it? How do you create a document? Once the document is created, how can it be kept for another day? Read on to find the answers to these questions.

THE WORDPERFECT SCREEN

Look at the WordPerfect working screen. You should see a menu bar at the top and a status line at the bottom. In the upper left corner of the screen is your *cursor*, the blinking line that identifies your location in the document.

SCREEN MODES

WordPerfect 6.0 for DOS enables you to work in one of three modes–Text, Graphics, or Page. The *Text mode* is the fastest, but it doesn't display your document the way it will appear when printed. It looks much like WordPerfect 5.0 or 5.1 for DOS–on a color monitor, the default background color is bright blue. It is great for keying and editing text. When you want to apply fancy formats to your text, you will probably choose to work in one of the other modes.

The *Graphics mode* is not as fast as the Text mode. The default is a gray menu bar at the top and a gray status line at the bottom. The background on the working screen is nearly white. When you work in the Graphics mode, you will be able to see full justification, graphics, and a better representation of the appearance of the final document.

The *Page mode* goes one step further. It leaves space on the screen for the top and bottom margins and enables you to see headers, footers, and footnotes along with your documents. This mode is the slowest, especially if you are working on a computer with a smaller or slower processor.

THE MENU BAR

At the top of the screen is the menu bar. The menus provide all of the choices for layout and a wide variety of WordPerfect features. You can access the menus from the keyboard by holding the Alt key while you press the highlighted character in each menu name, or you can point to the desired menu with the mouse and click the left mouse button. Doing so opens a menu that looks much like Figure 1-1. When the menu is open, you can choose menu items with the mouse or by keying the character highlighted in the particular menu choice.

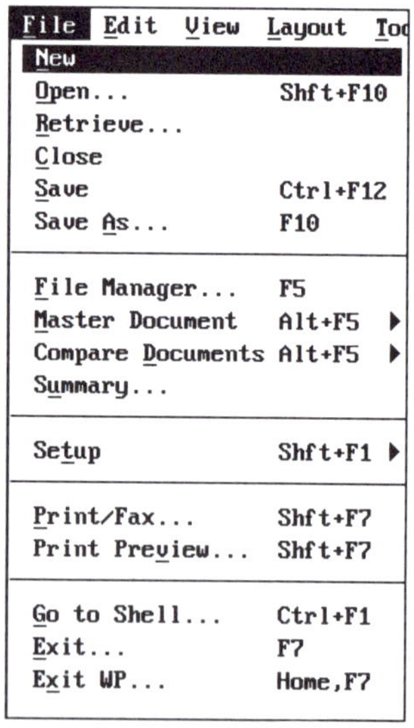

NOTE

The WordPerfect working screen should be showing on your computer when you begin this lesson. If it is not, please turn to Appendix A for instructions about how to start WordPerfect. You should also have a keyboard template listing the function key assignments which are coded in red, blue, and green for use with the Ctrl, Alt, and Shift keys and black for use alone.

FIGURE 1-1
The File Menu

2 LESSON 1 STARTING AND EXITING WORDPERFECT

1. Press **Alt-F** to open the **F**ile menu.
2. Look at the **F**ile menu. Note that one letter in each menu choice is highlighted or underlined. Keying the highlighted letter will choose that menu item. You may also choose a menu item with the mouse. You might also note that the function keystrokes are listed at the right for the menu choices that can be made without using the mouse.
3. Note that some menu items are followed by a right arrow (→). The arrow indicates that choosing that item will open yet another menu.
4. Note that some menu items are followed by three dots. The dots indicate that choosing that item will open a dialog box. Dialog boxes enable you to make choices and communicate with the WordPerfect program.
5. Choose **S**ave and look at the dialog box. It will look much like Figure 1-2. There is a place in the dialog box for you to key text (Filename), make a selection (Format), or make a number of other choices by tabbing to one of the other buttons (or choosing them with the mouse).

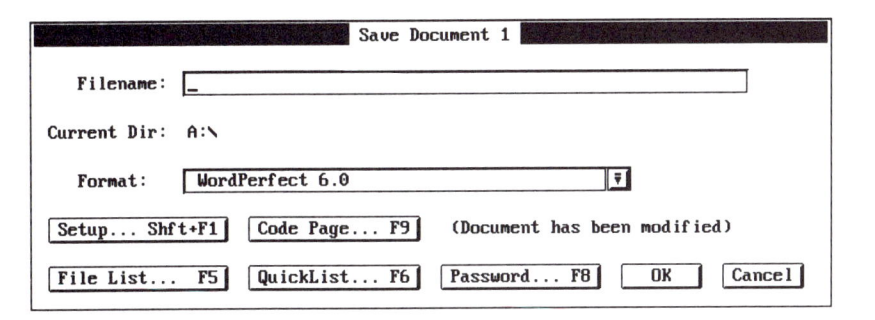

> **EXERCISE 1-1**
>
> Using the mouse pointer, point to **F**ile and click the left mouse button.

> **FIGURE 1-2**
> The Save Dialog Box

6. Press **Esc** twice to close the Save dialog box.

The menu bar may be used in place of the function keys for choosing WordPerfect features. Most users will use the menus for some choices and the function keys for others. You should have a color coded keyboard template showing what function keys to use for the WordPerfect features.

THE STATUS LINE

At the bottom left, WordPerfect reports the font in which you are working unless a document that has already been named is showing on the screen. If that is the case, the filepath and name of the document is displayed at the lower left of the screen.

At the lower right of the screen, WordPerfect reports your position in the document. The first information–*Doc 1*–reports which document screen you're on. You can have nine documents open at one time and can easily switch back and forth between them to copy or move text. The second piece of information–*Pg 1*–reports that you're on the first page of your document. The third piece of information–*Ln 1"*–tells you that your cursor is currently one inch from the top of the page. All four of WordPerfect's default margins are one inch. The final piece of information–*Pos 1"*–reports that your cursor is one inch from the left of the page. It is at the left margin. You will want to keep an eye on the status line. It provides you with lots of important information about your position in your document.

▶ **EXERCISE 1-2**

Press the **Enter** key (also known as the Return key) six times and watch the status line *Ln* setting change in sixths of an inch as it progresses to 1.17", 1.33", 1.5", 1.67", 1.83", and 2". The last line you can fit on the page before coming to the bottom 1-inch margin is 9.83". After filling that line, the next one will be *Ln 1"* of *Pg 2*. Use the **Backspace** key to return to *Ln 1"* of *Pg 1*.

▶ **EXERCISE 1-3**

Press the **Space Bar** and watch the *Pos* setting change to reflect the cursor position. Because the default setting for WordPerfect is Courier 10cpi (characters per inch), you will see the cursor progress reflected in tenths of an inch. Use **Backspace** to return to *Pos 1"*.

▶ **KEYING TEXT**

You are ready to key your first "document" using WordPerfect 6.0 for DOS. When entering text in paragraph form, use Enter only after the last line of the paragraph. Allow the words to "wrap" when a line is filled.

▶ **EXERCISE 1-4**

Key the paragraph in Figure 1-3. Use the **Backspace** key to correct any errors you make as you key. When you finish, keep the exercise showing on the screen.

| **FIGURE 1-3**

```
Perhaps more than ever before, American public education is
an issue of national concern.  Major studies have focused on
the weaknesses in our educational system, citing statistics
that appear to reflect a degeneration of teacher and student
performance.
```

▶ **CHECKING THE DRIVE**

Since the text you have on the screen will be lost if you exit the program, you need to save it on your disk. Before you can save it, however, you must be certain that the proper drive is set to receive your documents. Press F5 to see if the dialog box that opens shows **A:*.***, **B:*.***, or **C:*.***. The dialog box will look like Figure 1-4. You might have a different directory or drive designation than any of these. Press Esc to remove the dialog box.

4   LESSON 1   STARTING AND EXITING WORDPERFECT

FIGURE 1-4
The Specify File Manager List Dialog Box

If the directory that was listed is the place where you have your data disk, you are ready to proceed. If the directory shown is not where you wish to save your document, change to the correct directory or drive where you will save your practice documents.

NOTE

If you are learning in a classroom, your instructor will tell you where your documents should be saved. Usually student documents go on a disk in Drive A so they don't fill the computer's hard drive. See Setup in Appendix A if you need to make a change here.

SAVING TEXT

In WordPerfect 6.0 for DOS, you may save a document in a number of ways. You may press F7 for *Exit*. You may press F10 for *Save As*. Or you may choose **C**lose, **S**ave, Save **A**s, or **E**xit from the **F**ile menu. In each case, if the document has not already been saved, WordPerfect will ask if you would like to save the document. If you wish to save, you will need to name the document. If your document has already been saved, choosing Save **A**s will cause WordPerfect to prompt the old name and ask if you'd like to use the same name or give your document a new name. All of the other choices will cause the document to automatically be saved with the old name.

Save and Save **A**s allow the document to remain on the screen. All of the other choices close the document after it has been saved. WordPerfect 6.0 automatically backs your document up to a temporary file every 10 minutes so you won't lose too much work if the power to your computer is interrupted.

1. Press **F7** and save your document as **practice.1**. Press **Enter** after keying the name. When WordPerfect asks if you would like to exit WordPerfect, key **N** for No.

2. Key a little text on the screen and practice some of the other methods of saving and closing a file.

EXERCISE 1-5

Choose **C**lose from the **F**ile menu. Name your document **practice.1**.

LESSON 1 STARTING AND EXITING WORDPERFECT **5**

OPENING A DOCUMENT

Press F5. You will see the dialog box you looked at earlier that prompts the drive and directory WordPerfect thinks you might want. If it is correct, press Enter to open the File Manager. The File Manager displays a list of the documents that are on your disk. It should look like Figure 1-5. Use the arrow keys to move the highlight to the document you'd like to open and press Enter to open it.

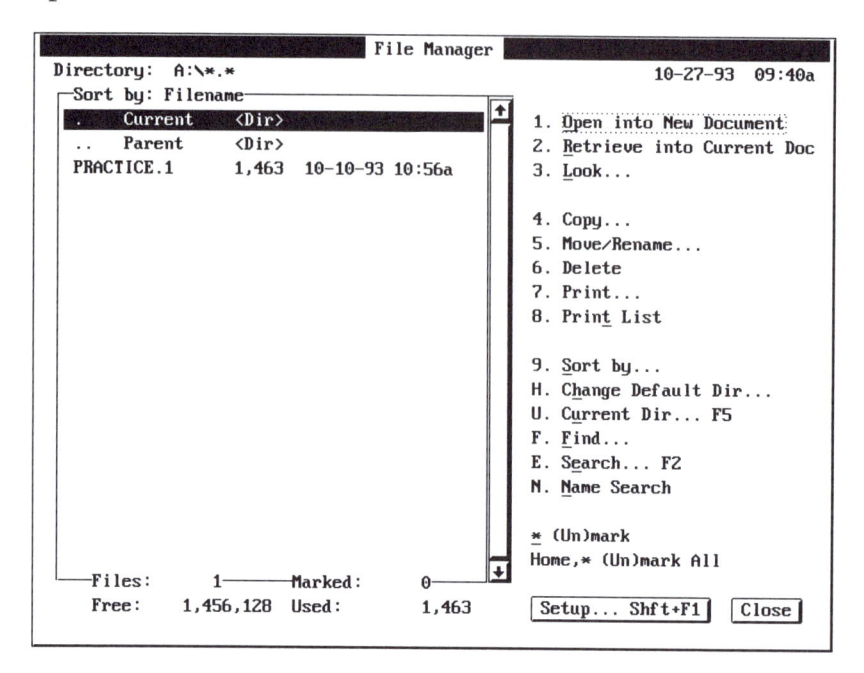

FIGURE 1-5
The File Manager

```
                         File Manager
Directory:  A:\*.*                          10-27-93   09:40a
 ─Sort by: Filename─
    .    Current    <Dir>              1. Open into New Document
    ..   Parent     <Dir>              2. Retrieve into Current Doc
    PRACTICE.1     1,463  10-10-93 10:56a   3. Look...

                                       4. Copy...
                                       5. Move/Rename...
                                       6. Delete
                                       7. Print...
                                       8. Print List

                                       9. Sort by...
                                       H. Change Default Dir...
                                       U. Current Dir... F5
                                       F. Find...
                                       E. Search... F2
                                       N. Name Search

                                       * (Un)mark
                                       Home,* (Un)mark All
 ─Files:      1────Marked:      0─
  Free:   1,456,128  Used:    1,463    Setup... Shft+F1    Close
```

Choose **O**pen from the **F**ile menu. Click **F5** for File Manager and then OK to open the File Manager. That's a lot of clicks. Pressing **F5** and **Enter** is MUCH faster, but the choice is yours!.

You can also *retrieve* a document. If you choose to retrieve, the document will be opened into the document you already have on the screen. When you *open* a document, it is opened onto a new screen. You can also open or retrieve a document using the Shift-F10 key combination. When you do that, you are asked to key the name of the document at the *Filename* prompt.

▶ **EXERCISE 1-6**

Open the File Manager. Use the arrow keys to move the highlight to **practice.1**. Press **Enter** to open the document. Note that the name of the document appears with the drive designation in the lower left corner.

6 LESSON 1 STARTING AND EXITING WORDPERFECT

RESAVING A DOCUMENT

After you've made a change or two in a document and wish to save it again with the same name, you may simply choose **S**ave or **C**lose from the **F**ile menu and the document will be saved. (**C**lose will also close the document. **S**ave will leave it open on the screen.)

If you wish to change the name of the document, choose Save **A**s. WordPerfect will prompt the old name and you can key the new name over it.

EXERCISE 1-7

Choose one of the methods described in the paragraph above to resave your **practice** document. Do not change the name of the document. Clear your screen.

SUMMARY

You have finished the first lesson. Congratulations! As a quick review of the WordPerfect basics, see if you can name the steps for each of the following:

Keying a paragraph

Saving a document

Opening a document

Resaving a document with the same name

LESSON 1 NOTES:

LESSON 2

Correcting Text

OBJECTIVES

Upon completion of this lesson, you will be able to:

1. Move the cursor in existing text.
2. Create a multiple-paragraph document.
3. Make simple corrections in text.
4. Paginate text.

Estimated Time: 1/2 hour

Since you now know how to create and save a document, it's time to learn to move your cursor in the document so you can make corrections, additions, and deletions. Moving the cursor efficiently will save you much time as you edit your documents.

One of the premises on which any word processing program is based is that you should NEVER key something over. You can fix, add to, delete from, and move text within a document. You'll learn about moving and copying text in Lesson 6. In this lesson, you need to concentrate on becoming proficient at moving the cursor and making simple corrections.

MOVING THE CURSOR

WordPerfect provides you with a dozen ways of moving the cursor in your text. As you experiment with them, you will find that some methods are much more useful than others. You will develop special favorites. Here is a list of the ways you can move your cursor without affecting the text:

↑, ↓	up, down one line at a time
←, →	left, right one character at a time
Page Down	forward through the document, from the top of one page forward to the top of the next page OR to the end of the text on a partial page
Page Up	backward through the document a page at a time, OR to the top of a partial page
End	end of the line
Home, Home, ←	beginning of the line
Ctrl→	beginning of next word
Ctrl←	beginning of previous word
Home, ↑	top of screen
Home, ↓	bottom of screen
Home, Home, ↑	top of document
Home, Home, ↓	bottom of document

When you use the Home key for the cursor movement listed above, you must first press the Home key, release it, and then press the appropriate arrow key. *Home* used together with *Ctrl* gives you the *Go to* function. *Go to* is used to move your cursor to a specific page. For example, if you had a five-page document and you wanted to go immediately from the first page to the top of the fifth page, you would press Ctrl-Home followed by 5 and then Enter.

You can also move the cursor with the mouse. Simply point to the place on the screen where you would like the cursor positioned, and click the left mouse button. You can also turn on scroll bars that help you move through the document. The horizontal and vertical scroll bar selections may be made from the **V**iew menu. With the scroll bars turned on, you can move the cursor through the text with the mouse pointer–clicking the up and down arrows and dragging the scroll box on the bar.

You can't hope to learn all of these cursor movements at one time. You will be instructed to practice some of them in this lesson. After you become more familiar with WordPerfect, you may wish to come back to this section to find out if there are more efficient methods of moving your cursor than the ones you are using.

▶ ADDING TO A DOCUMENT

We will begin this lesson by adding a couple of paragraphs to the document you created in Lesson 1.

Open **practice.1**. Use **Page Down** to move the cursor to the bottom of the document. Press **Enter** as many times as necessary so your cursor is a double space below the paragraph. Add the two paragraphs illustrated in Figure 2-1. Press **Enter** twice between paragraphs to separate them.

When you have finished keying the paragraphs, save the document as **practice.2** but keep it open on the screen for the next exercise. (You may save with **S**ave, Save **A**s, or **F10**. The document will be closed if you save with **F7** or by choosing **C**lose from the **F**ile menu.)

▶ **EXERCISE 2-1**

```
To offset this problem, teacher-training institutions are
lengthening their programs to five or six years in an effort
to better train their graduates for educating the nation's
youngsters.  Schools are using yearly performance
evaluations of instructors as the basis for increased pay.

On the student side, exams are required in many schools.
The exams are used to determine whether or not each student
is ready to progress to the next grade.  Many question
whether the exams are comprehensive and complete enough.
```

▶ **FIGURE 2-1**

▶ CORRECTING AND DELETING TEXT

WordPerfect provides you with two keys to correct little errors–the Backspace key and the Delete key. Both are equally useful, depending on the location of your cursor at the time you need to make a correction.

The Backspace key should be used for correcting errors to the *left* of the cursor. The Delete key should be used to correct errors at the cursor or those to the *right* of the cursor. Let's practice both of these methods for correcting errors.

1. Move your cursor to the last line of the paragraphs showing on the screen. Position it to the left of the the *e* of *enough*.

2. Use **Backspace** as many times as necessary to remove the words *and complete* along with the extra space between words. You may hold the **Backspace** key down to speed up the removal of many characters. (Sometimes you end up having to rekey some of the needed text!)

▶ **EXERCISE 2-2**

LESSON 2 CORRECTING TEXT **11**

3. Move the cursor to the space following the word *five* in the second line of the second paragraph. Use the **Delete** key to remove the words *or six* along with the extra space between words. Here, too, you can hold **Delete** down for longer deletions.

There are several methods for deleting bigger "chunks" of text.

Ctrl-Backspace   Deletes the word at the cursor

Ctrl-End   Deletes everything from the cursor to the end of the line

Ctrl-Page Down   Deletes everything from the cursor to the end of the page (WordPerfect will ask you if you REALLY want to do this!)

Larger chunks of text can be deleted using the Block feature. You will learn a number of things you can do with blocked text in Lesson 6.

Use the three-paragraph document on your screen and practice using the three commands above. Don't worry about destroying your text. You have it saved on your disk so you can open it again. When you finish practicing, use **F7** to close the document *without* saving and *without* exiting from WordPerfect. Learn this procedure for closing. You will be doing it often.

▶ **EXERCISE 2-3**

Choose **C**lose from the **F**ile menu.

INSERTING TEXT

WordPerfect is always in the *insert mode*. That is, when you key something into text that has already been keyed, everything moves over to make room for the new material.

The Insert or Ins key on your keyboard actually turns the insert mode OFF so that when you key, the new material takes the place of the old material. When you press Insert, the word *Typeover* appears in the lower left corner of the screen. It will remain there until you press the Insert key again. WordPerfect does some strange things if you accidentally leave Typeover on; so it is a good idea to turn it on, make the needed correction, and turn it off again.

Open **practice.2**. Move your cursor to the first line of the second paragraph, on the *t* of *teacher*. Add the phrase **a number of** by simply keying the words so the sentence reads:

" . . . problem, a number of teacher-training . . ."

Did you see the text reformat automatically? Practice adding and deleting text in these paragraphs. Again, clear the screen without saving.

▶ **EXERCISE 2-4**

EXERCISE 2-5

Open **practice.3** from the template disk, OR:

Key the text in Figure 2-2 exactly as it appears, including the misspelled words. Then correct the 12 errors (two in one word!) using the skills you have acquired. When you finish, save it with the name **practice.3** and clear the screen. (If you retrieved **practice.3** from the template disk, tell WordPerfect to Replace **practice.3** on your disk.)

FIGURE 2-2

```
More than 600,0000 people are avaiilable fer temporary work
on a daily basis, including routin secretarial, typing,
copuing, and mailing appplicationx.  But many can perform
specialized tasks involving word processsing, statistikal
tuping, legal suport, marketting, and other functions.
```

PAGINATING TEXT

You learned in Lesson 1 that the *Pg* indicator in the status line shows the count of the pages in a document. If you are using the default of six lines per inch, a page of text is filled when the *Ln* indicator reaches about **9.8"**. At that point, the *Pg* indicator changes to the next page, *Ln* returns to the **1"** designation, and a single line divides the screen.

At any time on a page, you can tell WordPerfect that you would like to begin a new page by inserting what's known as a Hard Page. This is done by holding the Ctrl key while you press Enter. A double line will appear across the screen. Try that a couple of times and watch the status line change from one page to another. Then backspace to return to *Pos 1", Ln 1"* of *Pg 1*. (Notice how easy it is to delete the hard page breaks with the Backspace key!)

SUMMARY

Look back over the lists of ways to move the cursor and the ways to make corrections presented in this lesson. As mentioned earlier, there are too many to remember at one time. As you work with your text, make an effort to try new ways of moving around in it. Think about saving keystrokes when deleting a chunk of text. With practice, you will become quite adept at moving within your documents and making corrections.

LESSON 2 NOTES:

ACTIVITY

LESSON 1 & 2 ACTIVITIES

LESSON 1

1. What four pieces of information are included in the status line?

2. How many menus are in the menu bar?

3. What choice must you make from the File menu to close a document?

4. What are the two choices of function keys you might use to save a document?

5. When do you name a document?

6. What is the name of the kind of box that appears asking for a document name?

7. What is used to indicate that a menu choice opens another menu?

8. List the steps to open a document you've saved on your disk.

9. After you've opened a document from your disk, the name of the document is displayed on the screen. Where is it displayed?

10. What happens when you use F7, F10, or Save As to save a document with the same name as one already saved on your disk?

11. When you are keying a paragraph in WordPerfect and you come to the end of the first line, the words that don't fit on the first line drop to the next line. What is this action called?

ACTIVITY 15

ACTIVITY

LESSON 2

1. List four ways to move your cursor UP in your document.

2. List the three methods of deleting text that require the use of the Ctrl key. What does each of them do?

   Ctrl-_____ Deletes:

   Ctrl-_____ Deletes:

   Ctrl-_____ Deletes:

3. If your cursor is to the left of the *P* in *WordPerfect* and you press Delete, what is deleted?

4. If your cursor is to the left of the *P* in *WordPerfect* and you press Backspace, what is deleted?

5. If your cursor is between the *d* and the *P* in *WordPerfect* and you add a space, between which two letters will the space be placed?

6. How do you begin a new page anywhere in your text? What have you inserted when you do this?

7. How can you tell the difference between a page break you've added to a document and one that was added automatically when a page became full?

8. Where must you position your cursor if you wish to add a paragraph to the bottom of an existing document? What key(s) will take you immediately to that location?

9. What keystrokes advance your cursor one word at a time? What keystrokes move your cursor through your text one screenful at a time?

Reference Question. Look at the Table of Contents in the *WordPerfect 6.0 Reference*. How many major parts are in the *Reference*, including the Index? Which section is the largest? How are the topics in that section arranged?

R E V I E W

Review exercises are scattered throughout these learning materials to help you reinforce the skills gained in the previous lessons. The time required for completion of these exercises is not included in the Estimated Time for the lesson.

Step-by-step instructions are not given for each exercise. See if you can complete the exercises without having to refer back to the lesson materials.

EXERCISE 1

Key the text in Figure 2-3. Press **Tab** before and after the numerals in each of the numbered items. When you finish, proofread, correct any errors in the document, and close it, saving it as **gifts.2r1**.

FIGURE 2-3

```
   1.   Flowers are acceptable in most cultures.  In many
countries you should avoid red roses because they signify
romantic interest.

   2.   Chocolates or gifts of candy are usually appropriate.

   3.   Gifts with company logos are usually acceptable,
providing the logo is small and unobtrusive.
```

EXERCISE 2

Key the short memo in Figure 2-4. After keying the word **TO**:, press **Tab** until the *Pos* indicator reads **2"** before keying **Mario**. Follow the same procedure with the rest of the opening lines. When you finish the document, proofread, correct, and close it, saving it as **tqm.2r2**.

FIGURE 2-4

```
TO:     Mario Mendez
FROM:   (key your name)
DATE:   (key the current date)
RE:     Self-Directed Teams

We're off to a good start with Total Quality Management
(TQM) in our organization.  Thank you for volunteering to
help with the initial planning meetings for our staff
training.

As you know, our goal for the future is to completely
convert our workforce to self-directed teams.  Your training
and former experiences in this area will be of great value
to our company.
```

REVIEW

EXERCISE 3

Open **gifts.2r1**. With the cursor at the top of the document, press **Enter** once and then ↑ once to move the cursor above the first item in the list. Key the short paragraph in Figure 2-5. Press **Enter** once more for a blank line.

Move the cursor to the end of the document and key the text in Figure 2-6. Remember to press **Tab** before and after the numerals in each item in the list. When you finish, save the document as **gifts.2r3** and close it.

FIGURE 2-5

> Customs vary around the world with regard to when to give gifts to business associates, what to give, and when and how the gift should be presented. Here are some general rules.

FIGURE 2-6

>   4.   To be safe, carry the gift in a shopping bag or someplace where it is out of sight. Hand the gift to the associate with both hands, never the left hand alone.
>
>   5.   In some cultures, the best gift is a dinner at a restaurant.

EXERCISE 4

Open **tqm.2r2**. Delete the entire second paragraph (can you do that efficiently?) and replace it with the text in Figure 2-7. When you finish, proofread, correct, and close your document, saving it as **tqm.2r4**.

FIGURE 2-7

> The first part of the plan for implementing TQM is to divide our employees into groups to train them about quality in an organization like ours. Plan to meet with me next Monday at 9 a.m. in my office. We'll set up a schedule for the first training group. Thanks for your help with this project.

LESSON 3

File Management

OBJECTIVES

Upon completion of this lesson, you will be able to:
1. Preview your documents before printing.
2. Print a document from the working screen.
3. Print a document from the File Manager.
4. Use the File Manager to manage your files.

Estimated Time: 1/4 hour

Now that you have become adept at creating documents and making simple corrections, you need to learn to make a printed copy (hard copy) of those documents. WordPerfect offers you several options regarding printing. Basically, you can print from the working screen or you can print from the disk. Either way, you have the option of printing the entire document or only a page or two of a document. Let's explore both methods.

PRINTING FROM THE WORKING SCREEN

Assume you've just finished the document and it appears on the screen. To print, press Shift-F7, verify that the correct printer is chosen, and press Enter to send the entire document to the printer. Before we try it, we need to take a look at the Print dialog box. Press Shift-F7 now. The Print/Fax dialog box should appear, looking much like Figure 3-1.

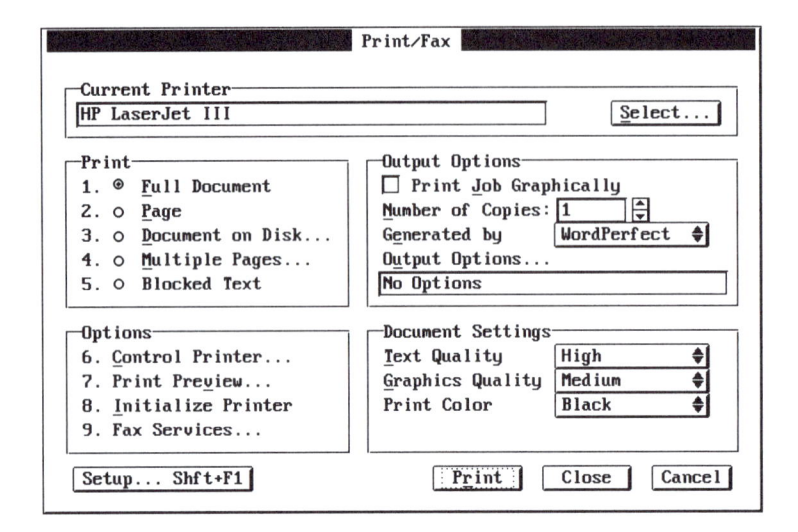

FIGURE 3-1
Print/Fax Dialog Box

At the top is the printer selection. If you have only one printer, that printer name should show here. If you have more than one printer, you may need to choose a different printer for different jobs. Just choose **S**elect to do this. Obviously, you need to be familiar with your printer before you can print a document. Since printers and printer procedures vary, it is assumed that you have a printer on-line to your computer as you work.

Notice that the **P**rint button at the bottom is chosen. If you are in the text mode, it is a different color. If you are in the graphics mode, *Print* has a dotted line around it. When the choice you want is chosen, simply press Enter to carry out the command. In this case, pressing Enter would send your document to the printer.

The Print/Fax dialog box contains some very important options. For example,2 **C**ontrol Printer allows you to check on the documents sent to the printer, interrupt a print job, or cancel a print command. Print Preview enables you to see your document in a reduced size to check the formatting before printing. **P**age enables you to print a single page; **D**ocument on Disk allows you to print a document without opening it; and **M**ultiple Pages allows you to print only selected pages (i.e., 7-10). You will want to explore the remainder of this dialog box on your own.

Close the dialog box by pressing F7 or Esc. Let's practice printing from the screen.

1. Open **practice.2.**
2. Press **Shift-F7** and then choose **7** Print Preview. Your document should appear in miniature, looking much like Figure 3-2.

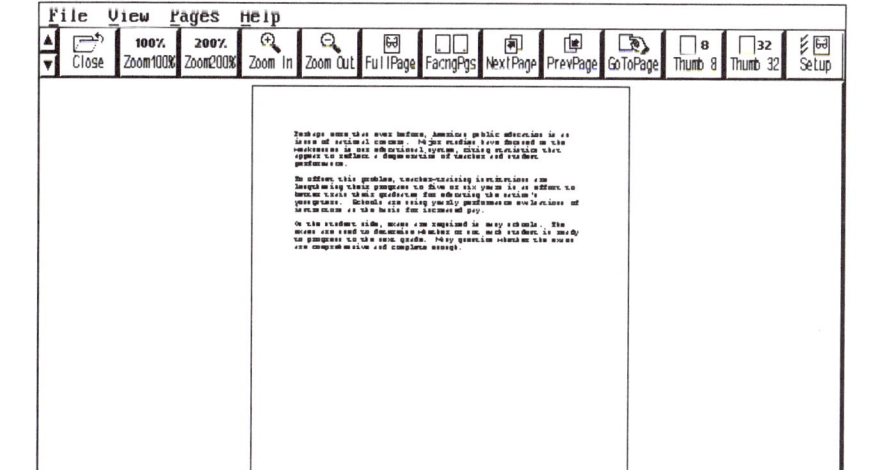

▶ **EXERCISE 3-1**

FIGURE 3-2
Document in Print Preview

3. Notice the Button Bar across the top of the screen, providing a variety of things you can do with this document miniature. (If the Button Bar doesn't show, choose Button Bar from the **V**iew menu.)
4. Press **F7** to close Print Pre**v**iew. Now press **Shift-F7** and then **Enter** to send this document to the printer.
5. Retrieve your hard copy of the document from the printer. Close the document without saving it.

▶ **PRINTING FROM THE FILE MANAGER**

When you print a document you have open on the screen, you must use the Print/Fax dialog box. You can also print directly from the disk. The File Manager includes a print option. Either method is equally useful, depending on where you are when you decide to print. Press F5 and then Enter to open the File Manager. It should look much like Figure 3-3.

Choose **F**ile **M**anager from the **F**ile menu and then press Enter to affirm the directory.

LESSON 3 FILE MANAGEMENT **21**

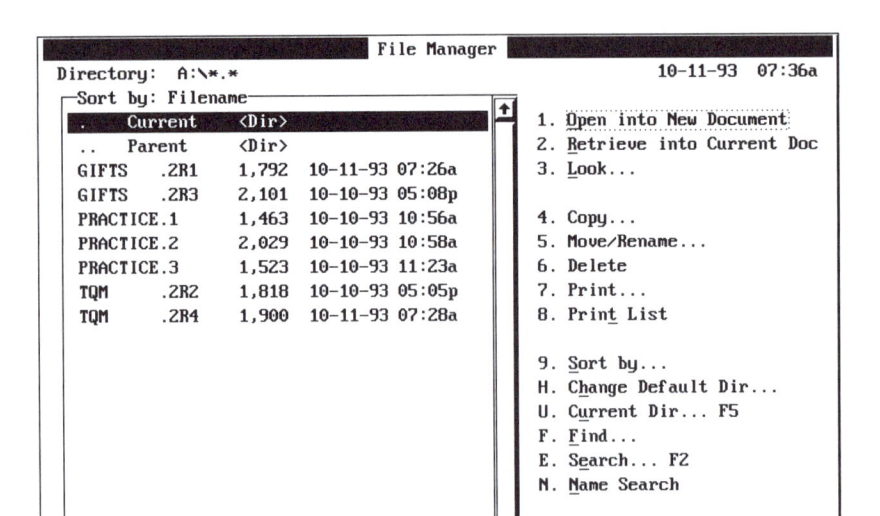

```
                    File Manager
Directory: A:\*.*                          10-11-93  07:36a
-Sort by: Filename-
      Current      <Dir>              1. Open into New Document
   .. Parent       <Dir>              2. Retrieve into Current Doc
   GIFTS   .2R1    1,792  10-11-93 07:26a   3. Look...
   GIFTS   .2R3    2,101  10-10-93 05:08p
   PRACTICE.1      1,463  10-10-93 10:56a   4. Copy...
   PRACTICE.2      2,029  10-10-93 10:58a   5. Move/Rename...
   PRACTICE.3      1,523  10-10-93 11:23a   6. Delete
   TQM     .2R2    1,818  10-10-93 05:05p   7. Print...
   TQM     .2R4    1,900  10-11-93 07:28a   8. Print List

                                           9. Sort by...
                                           H. Change Default Dir...
                                           U. Current Dir... F5
                                           F. Find...
                                           E. Search... F2
                                           N. Name Search

                                           * (Un)mark
                                           Home,* (Un)mark All

   -Files:      7——Marked:     0—
    Free:  1,443,840 Used:    12,626    Setup... Shft+F1   Close
```

FIGURE 3-3
The File Manager

To print, move the highlight to the document you wish to print and choose **7 P**rint. WordPerfect will ask which pages you wish to print. The default is **All**, so you can simply press Enter. Let's print!

▶ **EXERCISE 3-2**

With your File Manager showing, move the highlight bar to **tqm.2r4**. Choose **7 P**rint and press **Enter** to tell WordPerfect to print the entire document. Retrieve the hard copy (printed copy) of the document from the printer. If everything works, follow the same procedure to print **gifts.2r3**. If everything doesn't work, get some help with your printer before trying to print again.

▶ **FILE MANAGEMENT**

Open your File Manager again. At the top is information about the current directory or disk drive and the current date and time. At the bottom, WordPerfect tells you how many documents are saved on your disk, how much space has been used (measured in bytes), and how much space remains. While it probably won't happen with the documents you save from this course, it is possible to have space remaining on your disk but too many documents. Keep an eye on these numbers.

Note that listed with each file is information about the size of the file and the date and time the document was created. Your files are listed alphabetically, although menu choice **9 S**ort enables you to sort them by date, by size, and by a number of other choices. Just for fun, let's play with Sort.

1. Choose **9 S**ort by. A list of possible Sort criteria will appear. Choose **1 S**ort List by and then **3 D**ate/Time.

2. At the right of the dialog box, you are given the option of sorting with most recent FIRST or most recent LAST. Descending Sort would put the most recent at the top. Choose **3** Descending Sort. Press **Enter** or click OK.

3. Look at the list. The most recent exercises should be at the top, with the oldest ones at the bottom.

4. Now deselect **3** Descending Sort (just choose the item again), and sort the list again by **1 F**ilename.

▶ **EXERCISE 3-3**

The Sort in the File Manager is a neat feature. One use is that at the end of each day, you can sort by date. Then you can copy all of the documents created on that particular day onto a floppy disk as a backup.

Above the list of documents are *Current <Dir>* and *Parent <Dir>*. These may be used to move between directories. Instructions are included in Appendix A.

The menu includes quite a number of other choices. You can choose to **2 R**etrieve the highlighted document into the document you have open. (It will be inserted at the location of the cursor.) You can **4 C**opy a file from one disk to another, **5 M**ove/Rename a file, or **6 D**elete a file. Let's try **M**ove/Rename so you are comfortable with it in case you incorrectly name one of your documents and wish to fix it.

1. Position the highlight on **practice.1**. Choose **5 M**ove/Rename.

2. In the New Name box, key your own first name and press **Enter**. The original document will disappear from the list. Look in the alphabetic order to see if a document is there with your name.

3. Move the highlight to the document with your name and choose **3 L**ook to see if it is the document about American public education. (**L**ook doesn't open the document it just gives you a peek at the document.) Press **F7** to close Look and return to the File Manager.

4. Now choose **6 D**elete or press the **Delete** key and affirm the deletion. We don't need this document anymore.

▶ **EXERCISE 3-4**

You may wish to experiment with some of the other items in the File Manager on your own.

SUMMARY

In this lesson you learned two good ways to print your documents. Since hard copy output is usually the result of creating a document with a word processing program, this is a very important step in your learning. The File Manager, too, is very important. If you aren't good at managing your files, you won't be able to find the files when you need them. Be very certain you understand your print commands, your dialog boxes, and your printer.

LESSON 3 NOTES:

LESSON 4

Formatting Text

OBJECTIVES

Upon completion of this lesson, you will be able to:
1. Format characters and words, including
    a. Bold and Underline.
    b. Italics and Caps.
    c. Redline and Strikeout.
    d. Fonts.
    e. WordPerfect Character Sets.
    f. Dash Characters and Hard Spaces.
2. Format paragraphs, including
    a. Centering and Flush Right.
    b. Indent and Left/Right Indent.
3. Use the Reveal Codes feature.

Estimated Time: 1 1/2 hours

Up to this point, the only feature you've used to format your exercises is Tab, which you used to indent before and after the numerals in the **gifts** exercises. Now you will learn to change the way your text looks using a variety of WordPerfect features.

In addition, you will learn a quick way of finding the formatting codes that affect your document. Working with those codes makes editing easier. This is a longer lesson. You may not want to do it all in one sitting.

CHARACTER AND WORD FORMATTING

If your printer has the capability, you can use a number of ways to make words or phrases in your documents look different from the surrounding text. This can be done with various fonts, underlining, bold, capital letters, italics, redline, and strikeout.

BOLD

Bold may be turned on with F6, by pressing Ctrl-B, or by choosing Bold from the Font menu or the Font dialog box. That's a lot of choices, and the method you choose will depend on what you're doing. For straight keying of text, Ctrl-B is probably the best because it keeps your hands on the keyboard. If you are choosing a number of formats at one time, you'll probably choose Bold from the Font dialog box, along with the others. The font indicator in the status line tells you when Bold is turned on.

> **EXERCISE 4-1**
>
> Choose one of the methods listed above and turn on Bold. Key the words **WordPerfect Word Processing**. Notice that the words show in bold on the screen. Turn Bold off again, the same way you turned it on. Press **Enter** twice.

UNDERLINE

Underline may be turned on with F8, by pressing Ctrl-U, or by choosing Underline from the Font menu or the Font dialog box. When Underline is on, the *Pos* number in the status line is underlined if you are in the graphics mode or shows in a contrasting color in the text mode.

> **EXERCISE 4-2**
>
> Turn on Underline and key your name. The words will be underlined in the graphics mode. If you are working in the text mode, they will appear in a contrasting color. Turn off Underline and press **Enter** twice.

CAPS

Caps (all capital letters) can be turned on and off by simply pressing the Caps Lock key. When Caps Lock is turned on, the word *Pos* changes to *POS*. Some keyboards also have a light to tell you when Caps Lock is on. Caps Lock only affects the alphabetic characters. You must shift with the normal Shift key for symbols such as #, $, and %. If you shift and key alphabetic characters when Caps Lock is turned on, you will get lowercase letters. If you have something in lowercase that should have been all caps or vice versa, you can switch the case. Text must be blocked for this change. You'll learn this in Lesson 6.

Press **Caps Lock** and key your name. Return to lowercase, press **Enter** twice, and key your name again. Press **Enter** twice.

▶ **EXERCISE 4-3**

ITALICS

Italics may be chosen by pressing Ctrl-I, or by choosing Italic from the **F**ont menu or the Font dialog box. The font portion of the status line reports to you when italics is turned on.

Using the steps above, turn on Italics. Key the words
This line is in italic print.
Then turn Italics off. Press **Enter** *twice and key the words*
This line is normal.

▶ **EXERCISE 4-4**

Use **Shift-F7** *to print the document on your screen. Some brands of printers will not print in italic print. Instead, it will underline the italicized words.*

▶ **EXERCISE 4-5**

Save this practice exercise as **format.txt** *and close it.*

▶ **EXERCISE 4-6**

REDLINE AND STRIKEOUT

Redline and Strikeout are used to indicate text that is to be added to or deleted from a document. Usually text suggested for deletion is marked with Strikeout, and text suggested for addition is marked with Redline. Redline and Strikeout add another dimension to your document revision. When redlined text is approved for addition to the document and/or when the strikeout text is approved for deletion, you can press Alt-F5 and tell WordPerfect to add the redlined text and delete that marked with strikeout.

FONTS

You can add interest to your documents by varying the size and appearance of the type you use. WordPerfect 6.0 for DOS ships with a variety of scalable fonts that print graphically on most printers. These fonts may be chosen from the Fonts portion of the Font dialog box. Since that dialog box contains many of the choices you're learning about in this section, let's look at it. Press Ctrl-F8 to open the Font dialog box. It should look much like Figure 4-1.

Choose F**o**nt from the F**o**nt menu.

LESSON 4 FORMATTING TEXT **27**

FIGURE 4-1
Font Dialog Box

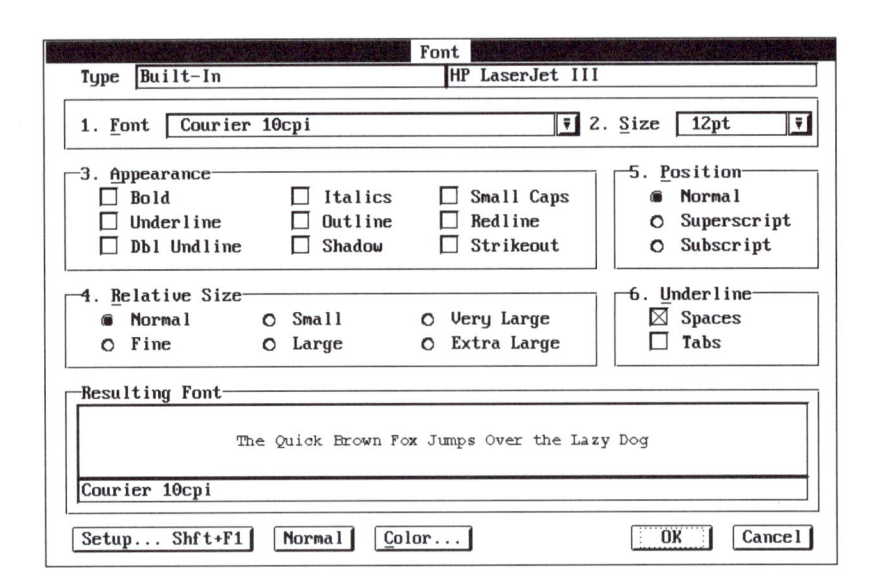

Just for review, look at **3 A**ppearance. Do the choices here look familiar? There are even a couple of extra ones with which you may wish to experiment. The next choice, **4 R**elative Size, enables you to increase or decrease the size of your characters by a set percentage. On the right, **5 P**osition allows you to enter superscripted or subscripted numerals to your documents. Beneath all of these is a window that displays the chosen font with the chosen attributes so you can see what the type will look like before you format your document.

This dialog box is also a good place to learn about choices you can make in WordPerfect dialog boxes. The choices that look like dots are called *radio buttons*. When you are making choices in a section with radio buttons, the choices are what's known as *mutually exclusive*. That means that you can't choose more than one. When you make a different choice, the previous one is deselected. On the other hand, the choices that have squares can all be chosen at one time (if you dare!). You can choose Bold and Italics along with Redline, for example.

Spend a minute or two making choices in this dialog box and looking at the results. Then return to all of the original settings.

▶ **EXERCISE 4-7**

Finally, let's look at the typefaces that are available in the program. Choose **1 F**ont or click the ↓ to open the pop-up list of fonts. Move through the list and look at the choices. Most are proportional fonts (where each character takes only as much space as it needs). The Type 1 fonts are designed primarily for postscript printers but will work slowly on most graphic printers. The Bitstream Speedo fonts are controlled by WordPerfect. The Courier 10cpi and 12cpi fonts are monospaced fonts that are standard on most configurations. (Courier 10cpi is the default font chosen by WordPerfect.) Any other typefaces that may appear in your list are made available by your printer.

28 LESSON 4 FORMATTING TEXT

Font sizes are measured in *points*. A 36-point font is approximately a half inch tall. The smaller the point number, the smaller the font. Business documents are usually prepared with fonts in the 10- to 12-point sizes. After you have chosen your font, choose **2 S**ize to select the desired size. You may change fonts as many times as you wish in a document. Each time you change the font, that change affects your document from the current position of the cursor forward to the next change.

▶ **EXERCISE 4-8**

Choose a font and size. Then return to your working screen and key your name followed by a double space. Return to the Font dialog box and make another choice. Key your name again. Do NOT try more than three fonts in this exercise. Many printers can't handle too many font changes.

When you finish, print your practice and close it, saving it as **fonts**.

FORMATTING AFTER KEYING

You will enjoy working with the formatting attributes covered in this section. Normally you will turn on the formatting attribute, key the text to be formatted, and turn off the attribute. Formatting can also be added to text that has already been keyed. To do this, you must first block the text to be formatted and then select the attribute. Lesson 6 covers blocking text.

▶ **WORDPERFECT CHARACTER SETS**

WordPerfect has a really neat feature that enables you to use hundreds of characters in your documents that are not available on the typical keyboard. This feature is accessed by first pressing Ctrl-w and then keying the character set number for the desired character. For example, you can put a real em dash (that's a printer's term for the dash used in the first line of the next paragraph) in your document by pressing Ctrl-w and then keying 4,34. (Key the numeral, the comma, no space, and two more numerals.)

There are a total of 15 sets of characters—designed for a variety of purposes. These character sets are illustrated in the *WordPerfect Reference* in Appendix A. Unless you do some unusual work, the one you'll use the most is Character Set 4, which is illustrated in Figure 4-2.

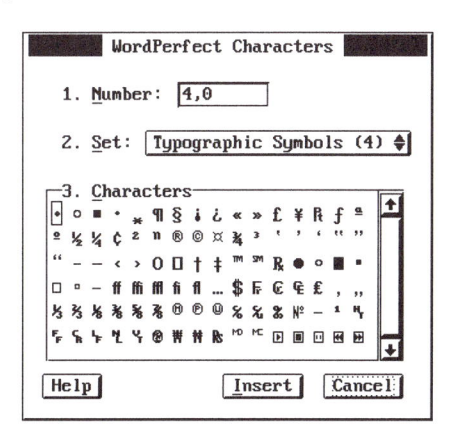

FIGURE 4-2
WordPerfect Character Set 4

LESSON 4 FORMATTING TEXT

As you can see, this character set includes fractions, smart quotation marks, bullets, and a variety of characters you might need for foreign languages. If you don't know the number of the character you need, you can press Ctrl-w, choose the appropriate set, and use your mouse to choose the appropriate character.

> **EXERCISE 4-9**
>
> Key the sentences in Figure 4-3. The numbers for the characters are given in parentheses at the end of the sentences. When you finish, print the exercise to see how the characters look. Then close the document, saving it as **char**.

> **FIGURE 4-3**
>
> ```
> It might cost $1.70 or more to buy £ of British money. (4,11)
>
> The cake was baked in a 350° oven. (6,36)
>
> "¿Dónde está su niña?" asked Carmelita. (4,32) (4,8) (1,59)
> (1,27) (1,57) (4,31)
> ```

There are also some shortcuts you can use if you don't want to remember the numbers. Here is a short list of some of the shortcuts:

½	Ctrl-w and then /2
—	Ctrl-w and then two hyphens
©	Ctrl-w and then key *co*
™	Ctrl-w and then key *tm*

There is no listing of the shortcuts. You can probably figure some of them out by yourself. If they don't work, you'll need to use the numbers.

▶ DASH CHARACTERS AND HARD SPACES

WordPerfect considers the space between words and keyed hyphens as acceptable places to end a line. Occasionally, you will want to mark some places as undesirable division points, such as:

- The hyphen or spaces in a formula,
- The space between the month and the day in a date, and
- The space between a person's first name and middle initial.

WordPerfect's solutions include two features known as the *dash character* and the *hard space*. Both of these features are accomplished by pressing AND RELEASING the Home key before keying the offending hyphen or space. (Note: Dash characters should NOT be used in compound words like twenty-five and mother-in-law.)

Look at Figure 4-4. This short paragraph includes two em dashes, a formula that requires hard spaces (to be keyed by pressing Home and then Space) between ALL of the characters in the formula, a minus sign (to be keyed by pressing Home and then Hyphen), and another hard space to go between the month and the day in the date.

▶ **EXERCISE 4-10**

Key the short paragraph in Figure 4-4, inserting em dashes, hard spaces, and a dash character in the correct places. If you don't do it correctly, you will probably end up with some bad end-of-line breaks. When you finish, print the exercise. Then save it as **spaces**. Keep it open on the screen.

FIGURE 4-4

```
The best formula—the one that will solve your problem—is
a + b - c = x + y.  The female scientist developed it on
January 1, 1924.
```

▶ FORMATTING PARAGRAPHS

WordPerfect has commands that you can use to center text, to align text at the right margin, and to indent paragraphs–from the left or from both sides of the page. In addition, you can do quite a number of things with tabs.

CENTER

The centering command is Shift-F6 or you can choose Alignment from the **L**ayout menu. When you give the centering command, the cursor moves to a point midway between the margins, and the text is centered as you key it. Pressing Enter ends center. You can center text that has already been keyed by moving the cursor to the beginning of the text to be centered and giving the center command.

Press **Shift-F6** and key the following line. End with **Enter**.

▶ **EXERCISE 4-11**

              This line is perfectly centered!

Now key the line again, beginning at the left margin. Move the cursor to the beginning of the line and press **Shift-F6** to center it. The line should align perfectly with the first line. Press **Page Down** and then press **Enter** twice.

FLUSH RIGHT

To align short lines of text at the right margin, use the flush right command, Alt-F6, or choose Flush Right from the Alignment portion of the **L**ayout menu. When you give this command, the cursor will move to the right margin, and the text will back up from the margin as you key it. The command is ended with Enter. As with centering, you can return to the beginning of the words keyed at the left margin and flush right those words.

EXERCISE 4-12

Press **Alt-F6** and key today's date, ending with **Enter** twice. Now key the date at the left margin. Return the cursor to the beginning of the line and give the flush right command again. Your dates should be aligned at the right. Print your practice and close it, saving it as **align**.

EXERCISE 4-13

Key the cast of characters in Figure 4-5. Center the title in all-bold capital letters followed by a quadruple space. Key the name of the character at the left margin and the name of the actor or actress flush with the right margin.

When you finish, print the document and close it, saving it on your disk as **fiddler**. If your paper is properly aligned, your document should have a 1-inch top margin and 1-inch margins on each side.

FIGURE 4-5

```
                           CAST
Tevye                                         Tim Riese
Golde                                        Pat Hanson
Tzeitel                                   Rachel Konkel
Hodel                                    Cindy Spaulding
Chava                                           Amy Hart
```

DOT LEADERS

You can add dot leaders between columns by pressing Alt-F6 twice. It's so easy!

EXERCISE 4-14

Redo the exercise in Figure 4-5. This time, after each character name, press **Alt-F6** two times. Then key the name of the actor or actress. When you finish, print the document and close it, saving it as **fiddler.dot**. Which version do you like best?

▶ INDENT, LEFT/RIGHT INDENT

WordPerfect enables you to temporarily change your left margin or both margins while you are keying text. This is done with the Indent and Left/Right Indent features.

→ **Indent** (F4) allows you to indent a paragraph from the left, just as this paragraph is indented. The text is indented to the first tab stop. The default WordPerfect tab stops are at each half inch. Indent is terminated with Enter, and you must press F4 again if you want another paragraph indented.

In research papers, long quotations are often single-spaced and indented one-half inch from both sides, as illustrated in this paragraph. The keystroke for this format is Shift-F4 (→Indent←).

If you press F4 followed by Shift-Tab (a back tab), you will get a format that automatically wraps and looks like this paragraph. It is called a *hanging indent* and is used primarily in bibliographies and enumerations. Let's practice some of these paragraph formats.

▶ **EXERCISE 4-15**

Key the short paragraphs in Figure 4-6, using **F4** for the second paragraph, **Shift-F4** for the fourth paragraph, and **F4** followed by **Shift-Tab** for the final paragraph. Use bold and italics as they are used in the exercise. Press **Enter** twice at the end of each paragraph. When you finish, print the document. Then close it, saving it as **indent**.

FIGURE 4-6

```
This paragraph begins at the left margin.  The words that
don't fit on the line are allowed to wrap to the next line
automatically.

   This paragraph begins at the first tab setting from the
   left margin because F4 was used to indent it.  Here, the
   words automatically wrap to a temporary margin.  If the
   paragraph is revised, the margins will hold their
   positions.

This paragraph begins at the left margin and is just like
the first paragraph. It is a normal paragraph.

   This paragraph is indented from both margins because
   it was begun with Shift-F4. This command indents the
   text to the first tab stop and an equal amount from
   the right.

This is another normal paragraph like the first one and the
third one.

This is a hanging indent paragraph.  It starts with F4 and
   then Shift-Tab to move the first line back to the left
   margin.
```

LESSON 4 FORMATTING TEXT

▶ REVEAL CODES

In this lesson you learned quite a number of ways of formatting your text. Each time you give a formatting command, one or two codes are implanted into your document. You can look at those codes to make it easier to edit your documents by pressing Alt-F3 or F11, or by choosing Reveal Codes from the View menu.

▶ **EXERCISE 4-16**

Open **spaces**. Reveal your codes now. The screen will split with a ruler dividing the top from the bottom. Find your cursor in the top portion of the screen. Find your cursor in the bottom portion of the screen.

1. Look at the [HSpace] codes in the paragraph. Move your cursor to the dash. The code should open up and display [–:4,34] if you entered it correctly. Make a list of all of the codes you can find in this document. Then close the document.

2. Open **format.txt** and look at the codes in that document. Add these codes to your list. Then close the document.

3. Do the same with **fonts**, **fiddler**, and **hyphen**.

You probably noticed that some of the features have an ON code and an OFF code. These are referred to as *paired codes* as opposed to the codes that appear only at the beginning of the text to be formatted, known as *open codes*. Paired codes can be removed from text by deleting either the On or the Off code.

When you get into heavy editing of your documents, you'll find that it is very helpful to be able to see when your cursor is within the pair of codes and when it is outside of the pair.

▶ SUMMARY

In this lesson you have used default settings to format your characters and paragraphs with quite a number of special formats. Two review exercises using some of these special formats follow the Lesson 3 and 4 Activities.

In Lesson 5 you will learn how to change the margin and tab settings, and you'll learn to work with the four kinds of justification.

LESSON 4 NOTES:

ACTIVITY

LESSON 3 & 4 ACTIVITIES

LESSON 3

1. List the steps for printing a document that is showing on your working screen.

2. List the steps for printing a document that has been saved on your disk.

3. What choice must you make in the Print dialog box to print a single page of the document showing on the screen?

4. How can you check on your current printer description?

5. When the term *hard copy* is used, what does it mean?

6. To what dialog box must you go to see how many documents you have saved on your disk?

7. Which dialog box tells you how many characters are in each document? How are those characters measured?

LESSON 4

1. On which portion of the WordPerfect working screen may you check to see if you have Underline or Bold turned on?

2. From which dialog box may you choose the font, bold, underlining, and italics? How do you open that dialog box?

3. List the steps to center your name using WordPerfect.

ACTIVITY 35

ACTIVITY

4. What is the name of the feature that causes text to be aligned at the right margin? How do you tell WordPerfect that you want that feature? What happens if you give that command twice?

5. What happens when you key a paragraph that you have indented using the F4 key?

6. Describe the keystrokes for properly keying the following formula: **a - b = c**

7. What is an *em dash* and how should it be keyed?

8. Circle the formatting commands that place paired codes in your document. Underline the commands that place open codes in your document.

Bold	Caps	→ Indent
Center	Underline	Fonts
Italics	Flush Right	Hard Spaces

9. What command must you give to tell WordPerfect you'd like to use the WordPerfect character sets?

10. At the beginning of every document created using WordPerfect 6.0 for DOS is a special code that formats the documents with the defaults. That code only shows when codes are revealed. What is the name of the code?

Reference Question. Look in the index of the *WordPerfect Reference* for the section on printer troubleshooting. What is the first question asked in the printer checklist? (Believe it or not, it is a valid question!) Look through the entire section. It may be of help to you sometime soon!

REVIEW

EXERCISE 1

Key the letter in Figure 4-7 according to the following instructions. When you finish, proofread it and print it. Then close it, saving it as **secure**.

Press **Enter** six times so the cursor is at *Ln 2"*. **Tab** to *Pos 4"* and key today's date. Press **Enter** four times. Center the subject line in bold. Use **Tab** and Underline to format the "disasters" as shown.

At the end, begin the closing and your name at *Pos 4"*, a double space below the last line of the paragraph. Separate the closing from your name by pressing **Enter** four times.

EXERCISE 2

Open **gifts.2r3**. Reveal your codes and find the [Lft Tab] code separating the first numeral from the word *Flowers*. Use either **Backspace** or **Delete** (depending on the position of the cursor) to delete that [Lft Tab] code. Press **F4** to insert an Indent code. Watch how the item reformats.

Follow the same procedure to replace **Tab** with **Indent** following each numeral. Print your document. Then close it, saving it as **gifts.4r2**.

REVIEW

FIGURE 4-7

(current date)

Ms. Reiko Onodera
329 May Building
Milwaukee, WI 53224

Dear Ms. Onodera:

        Subject: Protecting Vital Information

    Protection of an organization's vital information is crucial. There are a number of different kinds of disasters that organizations feel could never happen to them. One warning was the bank fire in Minneapolis in 1982 where the corporate headquarters of the bank were destroyed. Listed below are some of the disasters against which your organization needs to be protected.

<u>Natural Disasters</u>
    Fires and Floods
    Tornadoes and Hurricanes
    Earthquakes

<u>Man-Made Disasters</u>
    Sabotage
    Malfeasance
    Carelessness

    These are only the most obvious of the disasters that could destroy your organization's vital records. Our company offers experienced consultants-people who will work with your information processing department to protect you against loss of records in any of these instances.

    Please call me at the number on the letterhead to arrange for a consultation so we can talk about your needs. I can give you a quote, if you wish, for the price of our service. We would very much like to work with your organization to make certain that your vital records are safe.

                        Sincerely,

                        (your name)

LESSON 5

Changing Formats

OBJECTIVES

Upon completion of this lesson, you will be able to:

1. Cancel prompts.
2. Set and use decimal, center, right, and left tabs.
3. Change margins on all sides of the page.
4. Adjust line spacing.
5. Work with full, left, center, and right justification.

Estimated Time: 1 hour

WordPerfect's default settings are appropriate for many of your documents. However, there are bound to be times when you need to stretch the margins a little to fit more text on a page. There will be other times when your tabs need adjusting for just the right look, and changes in justification and line spacing will make your work easier.

WordPerfect 6.0 has a new feature called Auto Code Placement, which makes your formatting work easier because it eliminates the need for you to be so careful about the placement of the formatting codes. Page formatting codes are automatically placed at the top of the page. Paragraph formatting codes are automatically placed at the beginning of the paragraph. Then they format forward from that point.

All of the formats changed in this lesson may be chosen from the Format dialog box, which opens when you press Shift-F8, or they may be chosen from the **L**ayout menu. Some of the formats are found in the **L**ine Format dialog box, which may be chosen from either the **L**ayout menu or the Format dialog box.

Formatting codes are saved with your document on the disk. When you return to your working screen after closing a document, all formats have been reset to the default settings. When you open a document in which you made formatting changes, those formatting changes will be brought along with the document to the screen. Documents may have as many formatting changes in them as are needed.

CHANGING YOUR MIND

Before beginning your work with formats, it's a good time to look at the miscellaneous tools available to you for changing your mind. First, you already know that if you press an incorrect key, you can delete it with Backspace. If you choose formatting such as bold or italics and turn the format off again before keying any text, no codes will be placed in your document.

When you give a command that opens a dialog box or a menu, you can usually cancel the command with Esc (Escape) or F7 (Exit). Sometimes you have to press the "cancel" key twice.

Esc can also be used to *undelete* text. In fact, it remembers the last three things you've deleted so you can cycle through your deletions to find the desired text to reinsert into your document. Finally, WordPerfect has an *undo* feature which enables you to completely reverse the last change you made. You'll have ample opportunity to practice both Undo and Undelete in the next lesson.

SETTING TABS

To set tabs, you must go to the Line Format dialog box. You may do this by pressing Shift-F8 and choosing **L**ine, or by choosing **L**ine from the **L**ayout menu. Then you must choose **1 T**ab Set which opens the Tab Set dialog box. Do that now and look at the Tab Set dialog box. It should look like Figure 5-1.

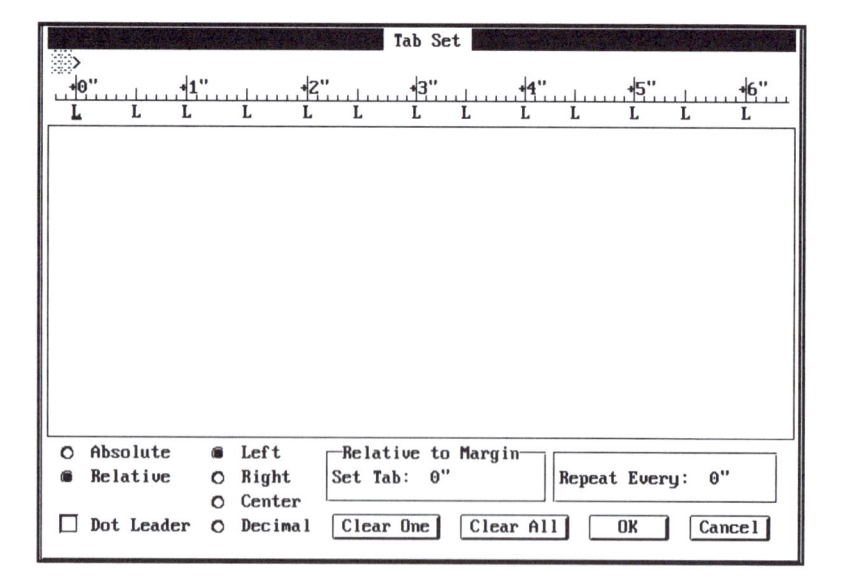

FIGURE 5-1
Tab Set Dialog Box

Look at the menu at the bottom. Notice that you can set **L**eft, **R**ight, **C**enter, and **D**ecimal tabs. The **L**'s in the ruler at the top are Left tabs and are set at each half inch. That's the default. Notice that the left margin is at 0". The area to the left of the margin marker is measured in negative inches and changes in size as you move the left margin. Because the margin is at 0", you don't have to reset your tabs when you change the margins. Here are some additional features:

- Clear **O**ne tab (Position the cursor on the tab and press Delete.)
- Clear **A**ll tabs (Key **A.**)
- Move the Cursor (The left and right arrows move the cursor one space at a time; the up and down arrows move the cursor from tab stop to tab stop.)
- Re**p**eat tabs (Set the tabs evenly across the ruler; just key in the increment, like 0.5 for half-inch tabs. Then press Enter.)
- Move tabs (Position the cursor under the tab to be moved. Use **Ctrl→** to move a tab to the right and **Ctrl←** to move to the left.)

Let's practice.

▶ **EXERCISE 5-1**

Choose Clear **A**ll to clear all of the tab stops. Then set new tabs at **+1.0"**, **+2.1"**, **+3.3"**, and **+4.4"**. Press **F7** and then **Home, F7** to return to your working screen. (**Home, F7** takes you out of several layers of dialog boxes all at once!) Reveal your codes and look at the Tab Set code. Add the code to your list and close the codes screen. Key the exercise in Figure 5-2. Begin at the left margin and use **Tab** to move from column to column.

When you finish, press **Enter** twice, proofread your work, and print it. Then save it as **colors** and keep it on the screen.

| FIGURE 5-2

```
red       blue      yellow    green     pink
gray      white     black     orange    chartreuse
brown     tan       gold      teal      mauve
```

▶ **EXERCISE 5-2**

Position your cursor at the beginning of the first line of colors and open the tab ruler. Press ↑ four times until the cursor is on the tab at **+4.4"**. Hold down **Ctrl** as you press → several times to move the tab stop to the right. If you go so far that *chartreuse* drops to the next line, use **Ctrl** ← to bring it back. Using the same method, reposition all of the columns by eye so they are spaced attractively. Close the document without saving.

TAB TYPES

WordPerfect gives you some choices about the kinds of tabs you use. We looked at the other three types when the Tab Set dialog box was open. Figure 5-3 shows how all four kinds of tabs can be used.

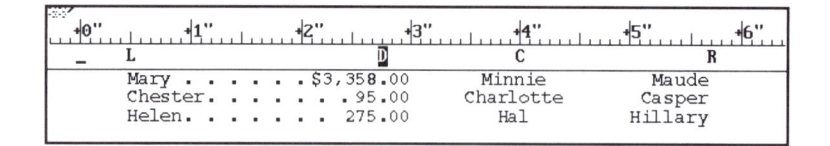

```
 +0"    +1"    +2"    +3"    +4"    +5"    +6"
   L             D             C             R
   Mary . . . . . $3,358.00    Minnie        Maude
   Chester . . . . . .95.00    Charlotte     Casper
   Helen . . . . . . 275.00    Hal           Hillary
```

FIGURE 5-3
Tab Types

- The **Left Tab** is used for things that need to be aligned at the left.
- **Decimal Tabs** are used to automatically align numbers, such as dollars and cents. A decimal tab is a **D** on the scale.
- The **Dot Leaders** were added automatically to the space between Columns 1 and 2. You can add dot leaders by choosing the Dot Leader box at the bottom of the dialog box when your cursor is on the tab that *follows* the dot leaders.
- A **Center Tab** may be used when you wish to have a series of things centered. Center tabs are represented by a **C** on the scale.
- When a **Right Tab** is set on the scale, anything keyed at that tab will back up from the tab. *Maude*, *Casper*, and *Hillary* backed up from the right tab at +5.25".

In all cases, you may key the numeral for the desired position of the tab and press Enter. Then you may either key **D** for Decimal, **C** for Center, or **R** for Right. The appropriate letter will take the place of the **L** on the scale. Or you can choose the tab type from the set of radio buttons at the bottom.

Set the following tabs for the exercise illustrated in Figure 5-4. The first column will be keyed at the left margin.

1. Set a **D**ecimal tab at **+2"** for the second column. Choose Dot Leaders for the space between Columns 1 and 2.
2. Set a **L**eft tab at **+3"** for the third column.
3. Set another **D**ecimal tab at **+5"** for the fourth column. Choose Dot Leaders. Return to your working screen.

Key the exercise. Use **Tab** to move from column to column. When you finish, save the exercise as **money.1** and keep it open on the screen.

▶ **EXERCISE 5-3**

```
Mary . . . . . . . $45.00       John . . . . . . .$156.99
Jo . . . . . . . . . 4.00       Sally . . . . . . . 3.25
George . . . . . . 375.00       Mai . . . . . . . . 1.65
```

FIGURE 5-4

MOVING TABS

Press Page Up to move the cursor to the beginning of the exercise. As you can see from looking at the document on your screen, the exercise isn't centered between the left and right margins. We'll adjust the tabs so the document will look better when printed.

▶ **EXERCISE 5-4**

Go to the Tab Set dialog box. Press ↑ until the cursor is at the **+5" D**ecimal tab. Hold **Ctrl** while you press → to move the tab stop to approximately **+6.2"** on the scale. Watch the document above the ruler to see the column move. Now move the **l**eft tab from **+3"** to **+3.5"** and the other **D**ecimal tab from **+2"** to **+2.7"**.

Return to your working screen. Print the exercise and close it, saving it as **money.2**.

▶ **EXERCISE 5-5**

Prepare a document that looks like Figure 5-3 (without the ruler, of course). Set the tabs and key the columns. Print it. Then close it, saving it as **tabtypes**.

▶ SETTING MARGINS

The WordPerfect default margins are set at one inch on all sides of the page. While you will rarely change the top and bottom margins, it is not uncommon to make changes in the side margins.

Choose **M**argins from the **L**ayout menu.

SIDE MARGINS

Side margins are a paragraph formatting function. Wherever your cursor is positioned when you give the command to change side margins, the code that results from the change will be moved to the beginning of the paragraph, and the entire paragraph will be formatted.

To change side margins, press Shift-F8 and choose **M**argins. Choose **L** for **L**eft and key the new setting. Press Tab to move the cursor to the setting for the right margin. Key the desired setting. When you are finished with the dialog box, press Home, F7 to return to your working screen. Your cursor will be at the left margin, and the *Pos* indicator will reflect that the left margin is now at the new position.

> **EXERCISE 5-6**

Set your side margins at **2"** on each side. Reveal your codes and look at the Margin Set code. Add it to your list and close the codes screen. Then key the paragraph in Figure 5-5. When you finish, print the document. Then close it, saving it as **listning.1**.

FIGURE 5-5

> One of the skills that needs to be developed in today's young people is the ability to listen. If students are being trained to work in an office, they need to be given exercises that help them to not only hear the instructions they are receiving from their co-workers but to comprehend and process the instructions in their minds so that they can follow through without error.

TOP AND BOTTOM MARGINS

If you wish to change the top and bottom margins, you will go to the same dialog box. The procedure is the same. Top and bottom margins are a page formatting function. No matter where your cursor is on the page when you give the command to change the top and bottom margins, the code will be moved to the top of the page and the entire page will be affected by the change.

Since changing the top and bottom margins is so much like changing the side margins–and just as easy–no practice is included.

LINE SPACING

Your WordPerfect documents will have single spacing unless you change spacing in the Line Format menu. Line Spacing is a paragraph format, so no matter where the cursor is in the paragraph when you switch to double spacing, for example, the entire paragraph will be double-spaced and the code will be moved to the beginning.

EXERCISE 5-7

Open **listning.1**. Go to the Line Format menu and choose Line **S**pacing. Change the setting to **2**. Return to your working screen. The document should now be double-spaced. Add the Line Spacing code to your list of codes.

Move the cursor to the bottom of the paragraph and press **Enter** so it is at the left margin, a double space below the last line. Return to the Line Format menu and change the spacing back to **1** (single). Key the additional sentences in Figure 5-6 to illustrate the change back to single spacing.

Print a copy of the document. Lay the copy aside to compare with your next exercise. Then close the document, saving it as **listning.2.**

44 LESSON 5 CHANGING FORMATS

FIGURE 5-6

```
A simple exercise is to divide the students into small
groups.  Read a set of instructions.  Then give the groups a
short time to reconstruct the instructions you read.  This
exercise not only teaches students to listen carefully, but
it also teaches them to work as team members.
```

JUSTIFICATION

Justification in a document has to do with how your text lines up at the margins. Go to the Line Format menu and choose Justification.

Left justification begins all lines squarely at the left margin, and the right side of your text is ragged. This is the default in WordPerfect 6.0.

Center justification centers all lines. This is useful on a title page.

Right justification ends all lines squarely at the right margin and the left side of your text is ragged. This format might be appropriate for display material.

Full justification begins all lines squarely at the left margin and ends all lines squarely at the right margin. Unless you are working with a proportional font, full justification tends to leave unsightly spaces between words.

Full, **A**ll Lines justification is like **F**ull justification except it even justifies short lines. Like **R**ight justification, this might be desirable for display material.

EXERCISE 5-8

Open **listning.2**. Go to the Line Format menu and change the justification to **F**ull. Return to your document and print it. Add the Justification code to your list of codes. Compare this full-justified document with the left-justified document you printed in Exercise 6. Which do you prefer?

Save the full-justified document as **listning.3** and close it.

LESSON 5 CHANGING FORMATS **45**

Go to the Line Format menu and choose **C**enter justification. Return to your working screen and key the lines in Figure 5-7. Print the exercise and close the document without saving. (Remember that all defaults are reset when a document is closed.)

▶ **EXERCISE 5-9**

```
                    (your name)


                   (current date)


          (the name of your school or company)
```

▍**FIGURE 5-7**

▶ CHANGING DEFAULTS

Some companies have preferences in formats that are different from those set by WordPerfect, such as different margins or justification. These formats can be changed permanently so that each time you start WordPerfect, the changes are in effect.

Instructions for making those changes are included in the Changing Defaults section of Appendix A.

▶ SUMMARY

There are quite a number of other formatting changes we could have practiced in this lesson. However, the most important ones include tabs, margins, spacing, and justification. Just think of how much you've learned already! You will get more practice in the following review exercise.

LESSON 5 NOTES:

REVIEW

Key the letter in Figure 5-8 using the following instructions. It will be a two-page letter. Don't worry about the second-page heading. You'll learn how to add one in a later lesson. Read all of the instructions before beginning.

1. Change the margins to **1.1"** on each side. Your line endings will be different than those in the figure.

2. Move the first tab stop to **+0.4"**. Do this by accessing the tab ruler, moving the cursor to the tab stop at **+0.5**, and pressing **Ctrl** ← once.

3. Place the date 2 inches from the top of the page. This means you should press **Enter** six times to add another inch to the 1-inch top margin. The *Ln* indicator will read **2:** when you are on the correct line. **Tab** to a tab stop near center to begin the date.

4. Press **Enter** six times between the date and inside address.

5. At the beginning of the first line of the enumeration, change to double spacing.

6. When keying the enumeration, use → **Indent** after keying each numeral and period so all lines are automatically indented as shown in the figure.

7. At the beginning of the paragraph following the enumeration, change back to single spacing.

8. Use **Tab** to position the closing lines at a tab stop near center.

9. Save the letter with the name **furnture** (misspelled, of course, to keep the name to eight letters). Print a copy and close the document.

> **NOTE**
>
> Choose **2** Insert Date **C**ode from the menu that appears when you press **Shift-F5**. The date will automatically be entered in your document. It will also be updated each time you open the document. If you prefer a date that doesn't change, you can choose **1** Insert Date **T**ext.

REVIEW

(current date)

Mr. Thomas Zeander
Zeander, Incorporated
2425 Seminole Street
Menasha, WI 54952-7890

Dear Mr. Zeander:

Thank you for your recent inquiry about our line of modular office furniture. As you well know, ergonomically designed workstations can increase efficiency in excess of 25 percent. When you consider the cost of salaries today, no one can afford to have uncomfortable employees in business offices.

I am enclosing a brochure containing all of the specifications for the type of modular furniture in which you are interested. The components included are:

1. A flat light-colored work surface measuring 24 by 60 inches. The work surface should be finished with a dull finish to eliminate the glare from any overhead lighting.

2. Acoustically treated sound barriers to separate one worker from another. These barriers need to be large enough so the workers have semiprivate office areas but not so tall that the workers feel claustrophobic.

3. An overhead shelf the same width as the workstation for reference materials and paper organizers. Also included are under-counter filing and storage areas, all within easy reach of the worker.

4. A task light attached to the underside of the overhead shelving unit.

As you know, of course, the most important element in any office is the chair. Our company handles a full line of ergonomically designed office chairs that you can mix and match with the other components of the workstation.

Please contact me if you would like to discuss your needs further.

                                        Sincerely,

                                        (your name)

Enclosure

FIGURE 5-8

LESSON 6

Editing Text

OBJECTIVES

Upon completion of this lesson, you will be able to:

1. Block text to format, cut, and copy.
2. Print and save blocked text.
3. Use Search and Replace.

Estimated Time: 1 hour

By this time you have become adept at correcting your errors by using either the Delete or the Backspace key and rekeying the material correctly. Sometimes, however, the incorrect text is too extensive to delete a character or a word at a time, or you may have simply keyed it in the wrong place. This lesson concentrates on working with pieces of text larger than a character or two.

Also included in this lesson is instruction in the use of the Search and Replace features. Search and Replace help you find and correct your errors. You will especially appreciate these tools when you work with longer documents.

BLOCKING TEXT

To work with a "chunk" of text, you must first select it. WordPerfect 6.0 calls selecting text *blocking*. There are many ways to block text with the keys on the keyboard as well as with the mouse.

FROM THE KEYBOARD

To block text from the keyboard, you must first move the cursor to the beginning of the text to be blocked. Then you must turn on Block. You can do this with either Alt-F4 or F12.

With Block turned on, move your cursor to the end of the text to be blocked–vertically or horizontally, and sometimes a combination of both. Block is turned off the same way it is turned on. Let's learn about Block by trying it. Each step below shows you a different way to block text, depending on what the text is.

EXERCISE 6-1

Open **practice.2**.

- **Using the Cursor**. Turn on Block. Press → as many times as needed to highlight the first three words. Turn off Block. Press **Page Up** to return to the beginning of the paragraphs to use the cursor a different way.

- **Using the Cursor**. Turn on Block. Select the first sentence by pressing ↓ once and **Ctrl** → as many times as needed to get to the end of the sentence. Turn Block off and return to the beginning.

- **Using the Space Bar**. Turn on Block. Select the first three words by pressing the **Space Bar** three times. Turn off Block and return to the beginning. (This works because text is blocked up to the first occurrence of a "unique" character. In this case, a space is the unique character. Try blocking up to the first *M*. Then return to the beginning.)

- **Using the Enter Key**. Turn on Block. Select the first paragraph by pressing **Enter**. Turn off Block and return to the beginning of the paragraph. (Here WordPerfect is searching for a [HRt] code.)

- **Using a Punctuation Mark**. Turn on Block. Select the first three sentences by keying the period three times. Turn off Block and return to the beginning of the *second* paragraph.

- **Using Page Down**. Turn on Block. Select the rest of the exercise by pressing the **Page Down** key.

As you can readily see, you can get creative with selecting text. Now let's see how to block text using a mouse and what we can do with the block once it is selected.

USING A MOUSE

If you have a mouse, the easiest way to block text is to position the mouse pointer on the beginning of the text to be blocked, depress the left mouse button, and drag the cursor to the end of the text to be blocked. You can drag the cursor vertically, horizontally, or diagonally. With practice, you'll be able to block your text much more quickly with the mouse than from the keyboard. To turn off the block, simply point outside of the selected area and click once.

You can also block text with the mouse by clicking.

- **Word**. Point to a word and click *twice* to block it.
- **Sentence**. Point to a sentence and click *three* times to block it.
- **Paragraph**. Point to a paragraph and click *four* times to block it.

▶ FORMATTING BLOCKED TEXT

After you have selected a block of text, you may:

- **Bold the Block** using one of the bold methods.
- **Underline the Block** using one of the underline methods.
- **Italicize the Block** using one of the methods for italics.
- **Change the Case** of the block with Shift-F3.

Formatting Practice. Practice blocking words, phrases, or sentences and formatting them with bold, underline, and italics until you are comfortable with blocking and formatting. Reveal your codes and practice removing some of the formatting from the document by deleting codes. You'll find that with paired codes like these, it doesn't matter if you delete the *On* code or the *Off* code. When you delete one, they will both disappear.

Block any three words in the paragraph and press **Shift-F3**. Choose **1 U**ppercase. Now block the same three words and change to Initial Caps. Block the last two words in one sentence and the first two words in the next sentence–all in one block. Change the block to uppercase. Now block the same words and change them to lowercase. What happened to the capital letter at the beginning of the sentence?

When you are comfortable with this kind of formatting, close the document without saving.

▶ **EXERCISE 6-2**

▶ DELETING BLOCKED TEXT

In addition to formatting, you can delete chunks of text with Block.

Delete Practice. Open **practice.2** again. Block the entire second paragraph and press **Delete** to delete the paragraph. Now block and delete the first sentence in the first paragraph.

▶ **EXERCISE 6-3**

Look at the two paragraphs that remain on the screen. When you work with blocks of text, you must be careful with extra blank lines. If your paragraphs are too far apart, move the cursor to a point between the paragraphs and press Delete to delete any extra lines. Sometimes you need to add lines between paragraphs. Just position the cursor and press Enter.

UNDELETE

WordPerfect remembers the last three things you delete, whether you block the text or not. If you delete something by accident, press Esc. WordPerfect will display your last deletion at the point of the cursor and give you the choices illustrated in Figure 6-1.

If you choose **1 R**estore, the deleted text will be returned to the document at the location of the cursor. If you choose **2 P**revious, WordPerfect will display the next-to-last deletion and give you the same choices. If you choose **2 P**revious *again*, the text displayed will be the third-from-last deletion. It will continue to cycle between the last three deletions until you choose **1 R**estore or Cancel. Let's practice.

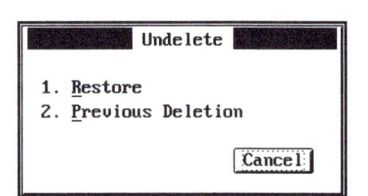

FIGURE 6-1
Undelete Dialog Box

Undelete Practice. Move your cursor to a spot midway between the two remaining paragraphs. If you need to, add enough hard returns so the cursor is on a line by itself with one blank line above and one blank line below it.

▶ **EXERCISE 6-4**

Press **Esc**. Unless you deleted something else since the last exercise, the sentence that appears is the sentence that belongs at the beginning of the first paragraph. You do NOT want that piece of text, so press **2 P**revious. The middle paragraph should appear. Choose **1 R**estore. If necessary, fix the spacing around the paragraph.

Now move the cursor to the beginning of the document. Press **Esc** again. The deleted text that is prompted should be the first sentence of the first paragraph. Choose **1 R**estore to put the text back in its proper location. (If your document is a mess, close it without saving and open **practice.2** again.)

▶ COPYING AND MOVING BLOCKED TEXT

Perhaps the greatest benefit in blocking comes from the ability to copy or move text to a new location in your document. When you *copy* text, the block is left at its former location and you can insert a copy of it at another location. When you *move* text, it is removed from its former location and reinserted at the new location.

When text to be moved or copied has been blocked, the procedure differs based on whether or not you have a mouse. From the keyboard:

- To *move* text, press Ctrl-F4 and choose **1** Cu**t** and Paste. Position the cursor at the new location and press Enter. (The text will be moved to the new location.)

- To *copy* text, press Ctrl-F4 and choose **2 C**opy and Paste. Position the cursor at the new location and press Enter. (The text will appear in both the new and the old locations.)

With a mouse:

- To *move* text, point to the block and depress and hold the left mouse button while you drag the pointer to the new location. Release the mouse button. Actually, the flashing cursor indicates the exact location where the text will be moved.

- To *copy* text, follow exactly the same procedure but hold the Ctrl key until you have released the mouse button.

WordPerfect calls this procedure "drag and drop." Let's practice. If you have a mouse, practice the exercises below both ways–from the keyboard and with the mouse–so you can decide which method you prefer. But before you practice, we'll learn about another wonderful tool.

UNDO

Another feature, almost like Undelete, enables you to reverse the last formatting change you made. This feature is called Undo, which is accessed with Ctrl-z. (Undo and Undelete can also both be chosen from the **E**dit menu.)

Undo and Undelete seem the same when it comes to deleting and restoring text, but there is a very important difference. With Undelete, the text will be restored wherever your cursor is positioned. (You can actually use Undelete to move a block of text.) With Undo, deleted text will be restored to its original location.

> **EXERCISE 6-5**

1. Block the entire first paragraph. *Copy* that paragraph to a location that's a double space below the final paragraph. You now have four paragraphs on the screen. (You may need to add extra hard returns between the paragraphs.)

2. Move the second paragraph so it is between the third and fourth paragraphs.

3. Choose **U**ndo to return the paragraph to its original location. (Press **Ctrl-z** or choose **U**ndo from the **E**dit menu.)

4. Repeat Step 2.

5. Move the first sentence of the first paragraph to the beginning of the new third paragraph.

6. Copy the *"Schools are using . . ."* sentence so it is the first sentence in the document. Fix the spacing so it is in a paragraph by itself.

7. Practice Copy, Move, Undo, and Undelete until you are comfortable with them. Then close the document without saving.

MOVING A COLUMN

You can use Move to move a column that is preceded by a Tab or →Indent to a different location. Practice as you learn.

> **EXERCISE 6-6**

1. Open **colors** and move the cursor to the beginning of the word *blue*. Turn on Block.

2. Move the cursor down to the end of the word *tan*. The document portion of your screen will look like Figure 6-2.

```
red      blue     yellow   green    pink
gray     white    black    orange   chartreuse
brown    tan      gold     teal     mauve
```

FIGURE 6-2
Blocked Columns

3. Press **Ctrl-F4** and press **Tab** once so you can key **T** to choose **T**ype. Change the setting to **2 T**abular Column. The blocked text will change so that only the blocked column and the spaces before it are selected. The Move Block dialog box will still be showing.

4. Choose **1** Cu**t** and Paste. The column will disappear and all of the others will move to the left.

5. Position the cursor on the *p* of *pink* and press **Enter**. Watch as the *blue* column is inserted in front of the *pink* column.

6. What happens if you choose **U**ndo? Try it a couple of times. Then clear your screen without saving this revised document.

▶ PRINTING AND SAVING BLOCKS

You can use Block to print or to save a portion of a document. With a block of text highlighted on the screen, tell WordPerfect to print. WordPerfect will ask you to confirm the request to print the block before sending the block of text to the printer.

If you wish to save a portion of a document, highlight the block to be saved and give one of the Save commands. WordPerfect will ask you to name the block of text and will then save it on your disk. You may practice these features on your own.

▶ SEARCH AND REPLACE

WordPerfect will search for unique character strings in your work. If requested, it will even replace those unique character strings with other text, with or without confirmation from you.

SEARCH

You can press **F2** for Search or choose Searc**h** from the **E**dit menu. When you choose Search, the Search dialog box appears, asking you to key the text for which you wish to search. Choose Search now and look at the options at the bottom of the dialog box.

- **Backward Search** is an option. The default is to search forward from the position of the cursor, but you can change that.
- **Case Sensitive** search has to do with if WordPerfect will find the words regardless of whether or not they begin with a capital letter.
- **Whole Words Only** can save you from a mess if you search for a word like "the." With the option deselected, you could end up with *weather, there, they, them, bother* and a whole lot of words that contain those three letters.
- **Extended Search** takes your search beyond just the text in the document.

Search is usually used to move quickly to a misspelled word or error. You will find many creative uses for Search. Let's practice.

▶ **EXERCISE 6-7**

1. Open **gifts.4r2**. Press **F2** and key **log** to search for *logo*. Press **F2** once or **Enter** twice to start the search. The cursor should stop at the end of the string for which you searched.

2. Leave the cursor where it is and do a Backward search for **rul**. (Simply follow the instructions in Step 1 but choose the *Backward* option.) Did it work?

3. Press **Page Up** (This is usually a good idea before a search. Then you don't need to worry about choosing *Backward*.) Search (forward) for the word **shop**. The cursor should stop in the middle of the word *shopping*. Press **Ctrl-Backspace** to delete it.

4. Keep the document open on the screen for the next exercise.

REPLACE

Replace is very much like Search except that it enables you to "replace" one word or phrase with another. You may confirm each replacement, or you may tell WordPerfect to go ahead and make all of the replacements.

Replace may be chosen from the **E**dit menu, or you can start Replace with Alt-F2. WordPerfect first asks what to search for and then asks you to key the replacement text. Let's learn as we practice.

▶ **EXERCISE 6-8**

1. Glance through the document and look at the variations of the word *gift*. Return to the top of the document and press **Alt-F2**.

2. Search for **gift**. Replace with **present**. Choose **3** Co**n**firm Replacement and **6** Find **W**hole Words Only.

3. Press **F2** to start the search. WordPerfect will stop at the first occurrence of the word *gift* and ask you to confirm. Key **Y** for Yes.

4. Repeat Step 3 until there are no more occurrences. How many times did you key **Y** for Yes?

5. Press **Page Up**. Press **Alt-F2**. Deselect **3** Co**n**firm Replacement and **6** Find **W**hole Words Only. (Remember, the whole words have already been replaced.)

6. Complete the search and replace. How many replacements were made this time?

Remember how many times you replaced the word *gift* with the word *present*. We're going to practice again. This time we will not confirm, and we will not limit the search and replace to whole words. This time we'll replace the word *present* with the word *gift*.

▶ **EXERCISE 6-9**

1. Return to the top of the document. Open the Replace dialog box. Tell WordPerfect to search for **present** and replace it with **gift**.

2. Be sure none of the options are chosen. Tell WordPerfect to make the replacements.

3. How many were made? Does that number match the total replacements in Exercise 7? Look through the document and see if you can identify the problem. (Read carefully!!)

4. When you figure it out, close the document without saving.

This exercise should help you to understand how careful you must be when you use Replace. Define the string of characters carefully so there can be no question about what you're requesting of WordPerfect.

Search and Replace can also be used to find and/or change formatting codes. The procedure is the same except that you must choose the codes from a menu that appears when you choose the Codes . . . F5 button at the bottom of the Search and Replace dialog box.

SUMMARY

This lesson on editing text has contained quite a lot of information that should be useful to you as you do your work. A big part of it was devoted to the *Block* feature and all of the ways you can use Block to make it unnecessary for you to rekey something in a different place or with different formatting. This saves keystrokes, and saving keystrokes is one of the basic purposes for word processing.

Search and Replace, too, are wonderful features. You can search for just about any word, phrase, or code in a document. WordPerfect will take you directly to it! What a big time-saver that can be.

LESSON 6 NOTES:

ACTIVITY

LESSON 5 & 6 ACTIVITIES

LESSON 5

1. List all of the keystrokes or menu choices necessary to clear all tabs and set a decimal tab with dot leaders at **Pos 6.5"**.

2. How many kinds of tabs can you set in WordPerfect? Exactly how do you add dot leaders between the columns of a two-column table?

3. You've learned that **Esc** can be used to clear something FROM the screen and that it can be used to restore something TO the screen. Describe these different uses of **Esc**.

4. WordPerfect margins are measured in inches. Is the right margin measured from the right or the left edge of the paper?

5. How many times in a document can you change line spacing and/or left and right margins?

6. Describe the five kinds of justification available in WordPerfect. Which one is the default setting?

7. Can you make formatting changes in a document after it has been saved on the disk and cleared from the screen? Describe the steps necessary to change the margins of a document you've already saved.

ACTIVITY 59

ACTIVITY

LESSON 6

1. Assume your cursor is at the beginning of a paragraph. Describe the most efficient *keyboard* method of blocking that entire paragraph.

2. Assume you wish to do something with a sentence in the middle of a long paragraph. What is the most efficient *mouse* method of blocking that sentence?

3. List five or more things you can do with a chunk of text after it has been blocked.

4. What is the difference between copying and moving a block of text?

5. Assume you have a multiple-page document with the name Christianson misspelled as Christensen throughout the document. List the steps for efficiently replacing the misspelled name with the correctly spelled name.

6. Assume you've discovered you deleted something from your document that you need to undelete. How many deletions does WordPerfect remember?

Reference Questions. Turn in the *WordPerfect Reference* to the section on Tabs. The page numbers in the Dot Leaders section are not properly aligned. What kind of tab stop might have been used for the second column in this sample to make the page numbers look better?

Turn in the *WordPerfect Reference* to the short section on Block. In the Helps and Hints section, it suggests you can use another feature you learned about in this lesson to define a block. What is that feature and how do you suppose this works?

LESSON 7

Writing Tools

OBJECTIVES

Upon completion of this lesson, you will be able to:

1. Use the WordPerfect Speller.
2. Use the Thesaurus.
3. Check your writing with Grammatik.
4. Use WordPerfect hyphenation.

Estimated Time: 1/2 hour

While the writing tools that come with WordPerfect don't help you format your documents, they do help you prepare documents that are well written. The Speller checks your work for misspelled words. The Thesaurus helps you find just the right word when you are doing original writing. Grammatik will look at your sentences and make suggestions that will make your writing more concise and clear.

In this lesson you will also learn some skills that will help even up the line endings in your paragraphs. The hyphenation feature is strictly cosmetic—it makes for a better looking document. Good looking documents are more apt to be read than ugly ones. Hyphenation is a continuation of the work you did earlier with hard spaces and dash characters.

THE SPELLER

The WordPerfect Speller compares the words in your document with those in a spelling dictionary. It highlights those that it can't find, one at a time, for you to decide how you'd like to deal with them. It will even give you a list of possible spellings of the words it highlights.

EXERCISE 7-1

1. Open **errors** from your template disk, OR:

Key the two paragraphs illustrated in Figure 7-1, making the errors as shown. Then save the document with the name **errors**. In this way it stays on the screen for the exercise, but you can open it again to practice the Speller if you'd like.

Now follow the steps below to use the Speller on the document.

2. With your cursor anywhere in the document, press **Ctrl-F2**.

3. Press **Enter** to affirm the default, **3 D**ocument. WordPerfect will start comparing your words with the words in the dictionary and will probably stop at part of your name. Since you undoubtedly keyed your name correctly and since you don't want the Speller to stop again at the bottom of the document, choose **2 S**kip in this Document.

   Choose **W**riting Tools and then **S**peller from the **T**ools menu.

4. WordPerfect will stop at *lerning*. Note that two possibilities for correct words are listed in the box at the left. You may key **B** to choose the second word in the list, you may move the highlight to that word and press **Enter**, or you may point to the correct spelling with the mouse pointer and double-click to put the word in your document.

5. WordPerfect will stop at *WordPerfek*. Surprisingly, it doesn't have any suggestions. You'll have to edit the word yourself. Choose **4** Edit **W**ord. This moves the cursor into the document where you may fix the error. Then press **F7** to resume the spell-checking of your document.

6. Work through the document.

   - *Houdini* is OK.
   - Choose the correct spelling of *completely*.
   - *Willbe* needs a space between the words—choose Edit and fix it.
   - Choose the correct spelling of *beautiful*.

7. Continue in the same manner until you come to the duplicate words. Choose **3 D**elete Duplicate Word. Then finish up the document.

8. Print a copy of the revised document and save it as **errors.ok**. Keep the document open on the screen.

FIGURE 7-1

```
    My name is (insert your full name) and I am in the
process of lerning to use WordPerfek at (insert the name of
your school).  When I am completly trained with this
software, I willbe able to create documents that are
beutiful!
    THis lesson is about the WordPerfect Speler.  The
speller will help me find my spelling erors so I can key
more rapidly in creating documents.  I understand, of corse,
that the speler doesn't eliminat the need for me to
proofread my documents because the Speller is is incapable
of identifying incorect words.  It just identifies incorrectly
spelled words.

(insert your full name)
```

You may have noticed that there were a few options in the Speller that you didn't use. You may work with some of them later in a different document.

The one option that you should NOT practice in the classroom is the one that enables you to add words to the dictionary. This is very useful on the job, because you can add your name, your employer's name, and the name of your company or city. If you do that, they won't be highlighted the next time the Speller encounters them in a document.

You may also have noticed that the default dictionary was listed at the bottom of the dialog box. WordPerfect enables you to create dictionaries of legal and medical terms—in fact, some are already available for people who work in those industries. It is very easy to customize the Speller for your particular needs.

THE THESAURUS

WordPerfect also provides you with a Thesaurus to help you find just the right word for your sentences. To use the Thesaurus, position the cursor on the word for which you wish to find a synonym. Then press Alt-F1 or choose **T**hesaurus from **W**riting Tools in the **T**ools menu and a list of synonyms will appear. Let's try it.

EXERCISE 7-2

1. Move the cursor to the word *beautiful* at the end of the first paragraph. Choose Thesaurus using one of the methods listed above.

2. Look at the list of synonyms (words that mean the same) that appear for the word *beautiful*. Move all the way to the bottom of the list. You will find a couple of antonyms (words that mean the opposite).

LESSON 7 WRITING TOOLS

3. Position the highlight on the word *stunning* and press **Enter** to open a list of synonyms for that word. (You can tell when WordPerfect has a list for a word because those words that have lists of their own have a dot or a bullet in front of them. Notice that the word *staggering* in the *stunning* list has no bullet.)

4. Move the highlight to the word *exquisite* in the second list. Then choose the **R**eplace button at the bottom of the dialog box to put that word into your document.

5. Close the document without saving it.

GRAMMATIK

Grammatik is a grammar checker that comes with WordPerfect products. You can use it for suggestions that may help you write more clearly. Let's try it on one of the documents you've already created.

▶ **EXERCISE 7-3**

1. Open **gifts.4r2** again. Go to the Writing Tools dialog box and choose **3 G**rammatik.

2. At the Grammatik opening screen, choose **I**nteractive Check.

3. Grammatik will first highlight *with regard to* and will tell you that it could be simplified. Follow the prompt to press **F2** for a list of simpler ways to say the same thing. Move the highlight to the word *regarding* and press **Enter** to choose it.

4. Press **F10** to move to the next problem. This one can be ignored for now. Press **F10** again to move on. Continue through the document, making appropriate decisions for the problems the program finds. Some of the messages are confusing, like the one about the *left hand*. Grammatik is obviously thinking about the word *hand* as a verb, not a noun.

5. When Grammatik is finished, the opening screen will again appear. This time choose the Statistics Check and look at some of the things Grammatik can tell you about your documents. When you've finished browsing, follow the prompt to return to the opening screen and **Q**uit Grammatik.

6. Print the revised document and close it, saving it as **gifts.7**.

HYPHENATION

In WordPerfect, words that don't fit at the end of one line are automatically wrapped to the next line because the default for hyphenation is Off. Sometimes that makes very ragged line endings when a large word is moved to the next line.

A solution to that problem is to use hyphenation. When you choose to hyphenate, WordPerfect's hyphenation dictionary helps with hyphenation to the point where you rarely need to make a decision about where a word should be divided. Let's practice.

▶ **EXERCISE 7-4**

1. Key the paragraph illustrated in Figure 7-2. Key the hyphens in the compound words as normal hyphens. Use an *em dash* for the dash before the example. Use hard spaces and a dash character in the formula so the formula isn't divided incorrectly.

FIGURE 7-2

```
Hyphenation is used to divide words at the end of a line
according to specific word division rules as taught in
communications skills and keyboarding classes.  WordPerfect
may correctly divide compound words such as sister-in-law,
father-in-law, self-esteem, and seventy-seven at the hyphen
when they fall at the end of the line.  Particular
attention, however, must be paid to special dash characters
and formulas with hard spaces—e.g., x - y = z.  Both must
be keyed correctly.
```

2. LOOK at your paragraph. Notice how short the second line is and how the compound words have been divided at the hyphen. Everything is OK so far, but hyphenation can make it more attractive.

3. Move the cursor to the beginning of the paragraph and block the paragraph. Press **Ctrl-c** to make a copy of the paragraph in memory. Then press **Page Down** to move the cursor to the bottom of the paragraph. Press **Enter** twice and press **Ctrl-v** to paste a copy of the paragraph below the original paragraph.

4. With the cursor somewhere in the second paragraph, go to the Line Format menu and choose **F**ull Justification.

5. LOOK at the second paragraph. Notice the unsightly spaces between words in the second paragraph.

6. Move your cursor to the top of the first paragraph and choose **6** H**y**phenation from the Line Format dialog box. An X should appear in the check box. Close the dialog box.

7. Now when you look at the paragraphs, you should see that *communications* has been hyphenated and both paragraphs are more attractive. If your formula isn't completely on one line, you did something wrong when you keyed it.

8. Print the document. Then save it as **hyphen** and close it.

If you decide after using hyphenation in a document that you don't like it, you can return to the Line Format dialog box and deselect H**y**phenation. The hyphens inserted by the program will be removed from the document.

LESSON 7 WRITING TOOLS **65**

SUMMARY

The writing tools covered in this lesson are all helpful to the person who uses WordPerfect.

- The Speller is useful to almost anyone who uses WordPerfect.
- The Thesaurus is most useful to people who compose their own documents.
- Grammatik helps the "composer" to make sure his or her writing is clear.
- Hyphenation simply helps to make your work look good.

LESSON 7 NOTES:

LESSON 8

Miscellaneous Tools

OBJECTIVES

Upon completion of this lesson, you will be able to:

1. Work with view document options.
2. Use the WordPerfect Ribbon.
3. Use and create a Button Bar.
4. Work with Bookmarks.

Estimated Time: 1 hour

In Lessons 1 through 6 you learned to create, save, revise, and dress up the appearance of your documents. In Lesson 7 you learned to make your documents more accurate.

Lesson 8 concentrates on a number of tools that help you use the program. The Ribbon, the Button Bar, and the different view document options all contribute to making WordPerfect a fun and easy program to use. Integrate the use of these tools into your everyday work with WordPerfect. You'll find that by using them you'll work more efficiently.

VIEWING DOCUMENTS

WordPerfect 6.0 for DOS provides you with a variety of options regarding how you see your documents. You learned earlier in the course that you can view your documents in the Text mode, the Graphics mode, and the Page mode. There are some other options.

ZOOM

Zoom can be chosen from the **V**iew menu or by pressing Ctrl-F3. If you choose it from the **V**iew menu, it looks much like Figure 8-1. Here you have a choice of looking at your document using Margin Width, Page Width, or Full Page. In addition, you can set the percentage of the size you'd like to see. No matter what size you choose, you are working with copy that can be formatted and edited (as opposed to Print Pre**v**iew where you can only LOOK). In addition, you can combine **Z**oom with the various modes like the Page mode where you can see top and bottom margin spaces. This helps you to evaluate the placement of your document on the page. Zoom in not available in the Text mode.

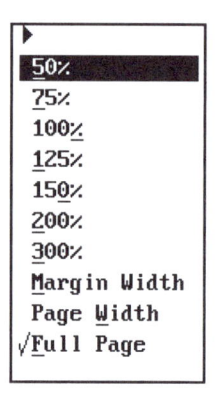

FIGURE 8-1
The Zoom menu

EXERCISE 8-1

1. Open **furnture**. Choose **Z**oom and change to **F**ull Page. Now change to the **P**age mode. How does the first page of the letter look?
2. Press **Page Down** to move to the second page.
3. With this document showing on the screen, experiment with **M**argin Width and Full Page. Try some of the **Z**oom percentages, ending with **M**argin Width.
4. When you finish, keep the document open for the next exercise.

WINDOWING

In WordPerfect 6.0 for DOS, you may have as many as nine documents open at one time. This is especially nice if you need to block chunks of text and move them from one document to another. The name of the document that has been saved is always displayed in the lower left corner of the screen, so you shouldn't have trouble remembering which document is which.

You can look at the list of documents that are open by pressing F3. The documents are numbered and you may simply key the number of the document you'd like to view.

As an alternative, you can tile the windows and look at small portions of all of them at one time or cascade the documents so you can move around among them. These features work best if you have a mouse. You'll use the **W**indow menu for most of them. You can access all of the choices from the keyboard, if you wish. The first choice in the Ctrl-F3 menu—Window—contains the windowing features. For this practice, no specific keystrokes are given. You may use either method.

▶ **EXERCISE 8-2**

1. The **furnture** document is still open. Now open the following documents: **gifts.4r2, fiddler**, and **listning.3**. Press **F3** to look at the list. Then use **Esc** to close the list again.

2. Go to the Window menu and choose **T**ile. Now all four of your documents appear at one time. Note the additional features of the "windows."

    - Each document has a dark bar (known as the *title bar*) across the top. The darkest one is the active window.
    - At the left of the dark bar is a little box. If you double-click that box (known as the *close* box), the document will be closed.
    - At the right of the title bar are up and down arrows. These are known as *minimize/maximize buttons*.

3. If you have a mouse, point to one of the UP arrows to maximize that document. The other documents disappear.

4. Tile your documents again. Point to one of the minimize (down) arrows. The document gets even smaller.

5. Click in the middle of one document at a time to activate that document. If you don't have a mouse, you can do the same thing by pressing **F3** and then choosing the document by number.

6. With a mouse, you can size and move the active document.

    - Move the pointer in the active document until it is on the title bar. Your pointer should become a four-headed arrow. Depress the left mouse button and drag the window to the middle of the screen.
    - Point to one of the side margins of the active document until the pointer is a two-headed arrow. Depress the left mouse button and drag the side of the window to make the document an inch or two wider.

7. Now choose **C**ascade to look at your documents in another way. You can move from document to document using the same methods you used in Steps 5 and 6.

8. For practice, block a sentence or a few words in one of the documents. Choose Copy with **Ctrl-c** and paste (**Ctrl-v**) the text into one of the other documents.

9. Experiment with the windowing features until you are comfortable with them. Then close all of the documents except **gifts.4r2** without saving them. Keep **gifts.4r2** open.

LESSON 8 MISCELLANEOUS TOOLS **69**

In this course you are mostly working with one document at a time. On the job that may not be true, and you'll really appreciate the windowing tools.

▶ THE RIBBON

The Ribbon is a tool that puts a number of the WordPerfect 6.0 features at your fingertips–IF you have a mouse. When the Ribbon is selected, it appears below the menu bar, and the top of your screen will look like Figure 8-2. Choose **R**ibbon from the **V**iew menu and click the arrow for each choice as it is discussed here.

| Wide ▼ | None | ▼ | 1 Col | ▼ | Left | ▼ | Courier 10cpi | ▼ | 12pt ▼ |

FIGURE 8-2
The Ribbon

- The first button is for Zoom. You know all about Zoom.
- The *None* button is for Outlining. You'll learn about that soon.
- The next button is obviously for Columns. That will be coming up soon, too.
- The *Left* button is for Justification. If you make lots of changes in justification, it's easier to make them here than to go to the Line Format dialog box for each change.
- The last two buttons are for typeface and point size of the type. The list of fonts available here should match the list available in the Font dialog box.

You may choose to work with your Ribbon displayed all of the time. Or you may choose to display it only for special kinds of documents. It takes only a little space from the size of the document on your screen.

▶ THE BUTTON BAR

The Button Bar is another tool that is much like the Ribbon because it makes tools more readily available. A mouse is also required for the use of the Button Bar. The major difference between the Ribbon and the Button Bar is that the Button Bar may be customized so that only the tools you use frequently are included.

Open the **V**iew menu and choose **B**utton Bar. If you see a message that says no Button Bar is selected, return to the **V**iew menu and choose Button Bar **S**etup. Then choose **S**elect. Look at the choices. There is a special Button Bar for such features as tables, outlining, macros, and layout. Choose *WPMAIN*. It is the default.

The Button Bar should appear across the top of the screen (below the Ribbon, if it is still displayed) and will look much like Figure 8-3.

FIGURE 8-3
Default Button Bar

Look at the choices available on the Button Bar. At the left of the screen there may be up and down arrows. If so, that indicates that the Button Bar contains more buttons than can be displayed on the screen at one time. You can scroll the Button Bar to the right or left with those arrows to make the remaining buttons available. Different size screens display the Button Bars differently. In Figure 8-3, not all of the buttons show. They might all be showing on the Button Bar on your screen.

You have some choices regarding how the Button Bar is displayed. Let's change the appearance of the Button Bar so you can see what options are available.

▶ **EXERCISE 8-3**

1. Choose Button Bar **S**etup from the **V**iew menu and then choose **O**ptions. The Button Bar Options dialog box should appear.

2. Notice that you can display the Button Bar at the top, bottom, left, or right of the screen. Note also that you can display the Button Bar with picture, text, or both.

3. For practice, choose to display your Button Bar at the left and display only text. Then close the dialog box and look at your Button Bar. It doesn't restrict your view of the document when it's at the left.

N O T E

Check with your instructor to see if you should just read this exercise..

The Button Bar may contain some features that you like and others that you don't ever use. So it's a good idea to build a Button Bar that's exactly right for your needs. We're going to create a Button Bar that might be useful to you in this course. We'll name it with your name. Before we can do that, however, we need to set up your location of files so the Button Bar is certain to be saved on your disk. Otherwise, if you work at a different computer, it won't be available to you.

▶ **EXERCISE 8-4**

1. Press **Shift-F1** and choose **5 L**ocation of Files.

2. Look at **2 M**acros/Keyboards/Button Bar. Two settings should be displayed there, and the first should be the location where your files are being saved as you work–probably Drive A.

3. If this hasn't been set, choose that option. A small dialog box will open that looks like Figure 8-4 if you are saving your documents on the disk in Drive A.

Choose Se**t**up from **F**ile menu and choose **L**ocation of Files.

LESSON 8 MISCELLANEOUS TOOLS **71**

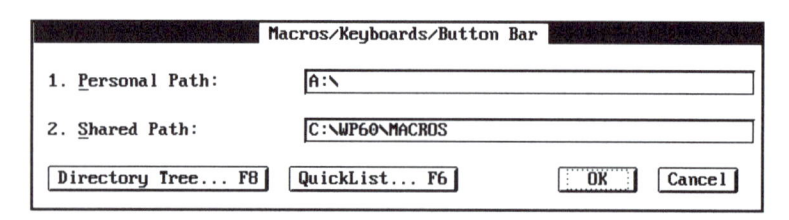

FIGURE 8-4
Macros/Keyboards/
Button Bar Dialog Box

4. Get the correct settings from your instructor. Make them, and then close the dialog boxes, returning to your document screen.

Now let's create and edit your very own personalized Button Bar.

▶ **EXERCISE 8-5**

1. Choose Button Bar **S**elect, near the bottom of the default Button Bar.
2. Choose **2 C**reate and name the Button Bar with your first name. A new dialog box appears with your name at the top of a very empty list. This is where you will insert the features to be included on your Button Bar. You can choose menu items or you can choose features. Since we can add most of the desired features from **2** Add **F**eature, make that choice.
3. Key **o** to move your cursor to the "o" section of the list and move the highlight to Open. Click the Select button or press **Enter** to add the feature to your list.
4. Choose **F** for Feature and add the following features in the same manner—one at a time. (The more you key of a feature name, the closer WordPerfect will get to it when searching through the list.)

Speller	Exit
Preview	File Manager
Print	Undelete
Save	Undo
Save As	Date Code
Close	Envelope

5. The Speller should probably be at the bottom of the list, since all of the features at the top have to do with file management. Let's edit your Button Bar. Position the highlight on *Speller*.
6. Choose **6 M**ove Button. *Speller* will disappear.
7. Move the highlight to the bottom of the list, just above *Envelope,* and press **Enter** to paste *Speller* into that location.
8. Click OK to close the Button Bar Edit dialog box. Your new Button Bar should appear. If it doesn't, go to the Select list and choose it.

72 LESSON 8 MISCELLANEOUS TOOLS

BOOKMARKS

One other small but useful tool in WordPerfect is the Bookmark and Quickmark tools. When you've had your codes revealed, you may have seen [Bookmark] codes in your documents. WordPerfect automatically puts a Bookmark into your document at the location of the cursor whenever you save a document.

Bookmarks can be named, and you may have as many different Bookmarks in your document as you wish. A Quickmark is generic, and each document may have only one Quickmark. How and why would you use these tools?

Quickmark. You are in the middle of editing a long document, and you have to put it away for the day. If you press Ctrl-q to insert the Quickmark at the location of the cursor before saving, the next day you may open the document and press Ctrl-f to move the cursor immediately to the Quickmark. Then you can pick up the editing where you left off.

Bookmark. Since Bookmarks must be named, you might put a Bookmark named *Joe* in the document so that when Joe is reading the report, he can look at the spot you've marked for him. If you don't like using personal names for Bookmarks, you can use anything you'd like. You may not, however, use the same Bookmark name twice in one document. Let's try a little Bookmark activity.

EXERCISE 8-6

Choose Boo**k**mark from the **E**dit menu.

1. Do you still have **gifts.4r2** open? If not, open it and position the cursor just to the right of the word *associates* on the second line.
2. Press **Shift-F12** to open the Bookmark dialog box.
3. Choose **3 C**reate and name the Bookmark **Joe**. Return to your document.
4. Follow the same procedure to put a Bookmark named **Janie** by the word *chocolates* (any idea why?) and one named **Robert** by the word *dinner* in the last item.
5. Press **Shift-F12** and move the highlight to *Janie*. Choose **1 F**ind. Did the cursor move to *chocolates*?
6. Save the document as **gifts.8** and close it. You might want to open it tomorrow and see if the cursor will move to *dinner* if you search for the *Robert* Bookmark.

LESSON 8 MISCELLANEOUS TOOLS

SUMMARY

This lesson contained some miscellaneous but useful tools. You learned a variety of ways of looking at your document(s). You also experimented with the Ribbon and the Button Bar. These features both save you from repetitive use of the function keys and the pull-down menus. Finally, you learned that Bookmarks help you to move quickly to a particular place in a document. Remember to use these tools in your work as you continue to learn about WordPerfect.

LESSON 8 NOTES:

ACTIVITY

▶ LESSON 7 & 8 ACTIVITIES

LESSON 7

1. Why must you proofread your documents even when you check them with the WordPerfect Speller?

2. What should you do when you are using WordPerfect on the job if the Speller highlights the name of your boss and your hometown?

3. How do you tell WordPerfect to replace the incorrectly spelled word with the correctly spelled one from the list?

4. What choice must you make in the WordPerfect Speller if you wish to look up the spelling of a single word?

5. What is the difference in the Speller between choosing Skip Once and Skip in this Document?

6. If you wish to look up a word in the WordPerfect Thesaurus, how do you tell WordPerfect which word to look up?

7. What are your options when Grammatik finds a grammar error in your document?

8. Why would anyone want to use hyphenation?

ACTIVITY

LESSON 8

1. What is the difference between viewing a document in the Graphics mode and viewing it in the Page mode?

2. What is the difference between choosing Page Width from Zoom or choosing Margin Width?

3. Which allows you to see the text of several documents at one time, Cascade or Tile?

4. List the features on the Ribbon that you've already learned to use.

5. Circle the choice that will allow you to see more buttons on your Button Bar: a) pictures and text at the left; b) pictures and text at the top; c) text only at the left; d) text only at the top.

6. What are the names of some of the other Button Bars that come with WordPerfect?

7. What is the difference between a Quickmark and a Bookmark?

Reference Question. Turn in the *WordPerfect Reference* to the section about the Ribbon. Study the dialog box illustrated in the Displaying the Ribbon Automatically section. What are the six categories of features that can be adjusted from this dialog box?

LESSON 9

WordPerfect Tables

OBJECTIVES

Upon completion of this lesson, you will be able to:

1. Discuss WordPerfect table terminology.
2. Create and format a table using the WordPerfect 6.0 Tables feature.
3. Use a table as a spreadsheet feature.

Estimated Time: 2 hours

The WordPerfect Tables feature helps you put your information into columns. When you are preparing your tables, graphic lines divide the information into a grid that looks something like Figure 9-1.

FIGURE 9-1
The Table Grid

This Tables feature not only helps you align your information, it also is a useful tool for formatting your columns and dressing them up so people can't wait to read the documents you prepare. Working with Tables looks hard at first. However, once you catch on, you'll find Tables to be great fun.

We'll begin by learning some of the terminology that goes along with your work with Tables.

TERMINOLOGY

A WordPerfect table is actually a spreadsheet. Here are some terms that are peculiar to the use of tables and spreadsheets.

Spreadsheet. A *spreadsheet* is a grid made up of columns and rows. The columns and rows may contain data or formulas used for financial purposes.

Columns. Vertical collections of information are called *columns*. Columns are labeled with letters (e.g., A, B, C).

Rows. Information is arranged horizontally into *rows*. Rows are labeled with numbers.

Cells. The point at which a row meets a column is called a *cell*. Each cell is said to have an *address* that identifies the column and row where the cell is located. For example, the cell where Column B meets Row 3 is called B3. This information is reported in WordPerfect at the beginning of the status line.

CREATE A TABLE

Let's practice as you learn. We'll create a simple table and put some text in the columns. When you finish, your table will look somewhat like the one in Figure 9-2. Read through ALL of the instructions in the exercise before beginning.

FIGURE 9-2
A WordPerfect Table

Salesperson	First	Second	Mid-Year
Johnnie Jacks	$499.25	$540.00	$1,039.25
Phillipe Darling	$1,035.89	$648.23	$1,684.12
Yang Lin	$625.88	$569.12	$1,195.00
Esther Flores	$385.90	$495.40	$881.30
Diane Jones	$485.00	$1,146.50	$1,631.50
Totals	$3,031.92	$3,399.25	$6,431.17

QUARTERLY AND MID-YEAR SALES EARNINGS

EXERCISE 9-1

1. Press **Alt-F7** for the Columns/Tables dialog box. Choose **2 T**ables and then **1 C**reate.

2. A small dialog box will ask how many columns and how many rows. The finished table will be larger, but we'll purposely begin with a table that is too small so you can practice increasing the size of a table. This table will have 3 columns and 3 rows. Fill in the numbers and click OK. The grid will appear, and you are in what's known as the table editor.

3. Study the menu at the bottom. We'll work with it shortly.

4. Use **Tab** and **Shift-Tab** to move around in the table. Return the cursor to Cell A1 and press **F7** to close the table editor.

Choose **T**ables and **C**reate from the Layout menu.

5. Key the text illustrated in Figure 9-3 into the table. Press **Tab** to move from cell to cell–even from the end of one row to the beginning of the next. Do NOT press **Enter** anywhere in the table. (If you press **Enter** by accident, you can backspace to remove the [HRt] code.) When you fill the last cell (C3), press **Tab** again. WordPerfect will add another row to your table for you.

6. When you finish keying, save your table as **table.1**. Keep it open.

```
Johnnie Jacks       499.25      540.00
Phillipe Darling     35.89      648.23
Yang Lin            625.88      569.12
Esther Flores       385.90      495.40
Diana Jones         485.00    1,146.50
```

FIGURE 9-3

As you can see, the Tables feature is different from setting up a traditional tabulation problem in a number of ways:

- You didn't have to do any figuring or setting of tabs. The columns were automatically set up for you.

- The columns were set up evenly. If the information you keyed into them had been more irregular in size, the spacing between columns would have been quite uneven. However, the column size can be adjusted quite easily.

- The columns extend to your margins. This, too, is an option that can be changed.

▶ EDIT AND FORMAT A TABLE

In the next series of exercises, you will be adding to the table and formatting it. These steps will take you through a number of menus in the table editor. Look at the other options as you go.

Insert and format columns and rows:

1. Move the cursor to Cell A1. Press **Alt-F11** to return to the table editor.

2. Note the Ins button in the table editor. Click the button, press **Insert**, or key **I** to tell WordPerfect to insert something. The dialog box illustrated in Figure 9-4 will appear. Choose **2 R**ows and change **3 H**ow many to **2**. Note the setting that says the rows will be inserted before the cursor. That's good. These will be heading rows.

3. When you are finished, click OK or press **Enter** to close the dialog box. Your table should now have two extra rows on top.

4. Position the cursor in Cell C3 and press **Insert** again. This time insert *one* column *after* the cursor. The columns will not be evenly spaced.

▶ **EXERCISE 9-2**

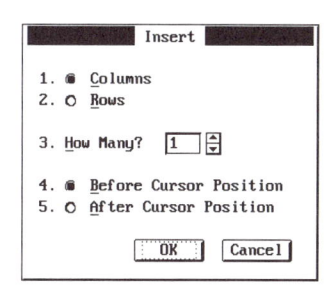

FIGURE 9-4
Insert Dialog Box

LESSON 9 WORDPERFECT TABLES **79**

5. Move the cursor to Cell A1. Press **F12** to turn on Block and press → three times to block all of Row 1. Choose **7 J**oin and key **Y** to affirm the joining.

6. Turn on Block and press ↓ once to block Rows 1 and 2 together.

7. Choose **1 C**ell. In the Cell Format dialog box, choose **4 J**ustification and **2 C**enter. Press **Enter** or click OK. Then press **F7** to exit from the table editor.

8. Key the heading information illustrated in Figure 9-5. Remember to use **Tab** to move from cell to cell.

9. Do an interim save of your table, naming it **table.2**. Keep it open.

QUARTERLY AND MID-YEAR SALES EARNINGS			
Salesperson	First	Second	Mid-Year

FIGURE 9-5

How does your table look so far? The dollar amounts don't look very good aligned as they are at the left of the columns. We'll format all three number columns, even though Column D is still empty. We'll also add a row for totals at the bottom of the table.

Format number columns and add a totals row:

1. Press **Alt-F11** to return to the table editor and move the cursor to Cell B3. Turn on Block and press **Page Down**. The three number columns should be blocked.

2. Choose **1 C**ell. In the Cell Format dialog box, first choose **6** Number **T**ype and choose **5 C**urrency. Press **Enter**.

3. Choose **4 J**ustification and then **6 D**ecimal Align. Press **Enter**. Notice that dollar signs were added to your numbers and that they are appropriately aligned.

4. Move the cursor to the column containing the names. Hold **Ctrl** while you press ← until the column is snug around *Phillipe Darling*. (If you go too far, you can reverse the process with **Ctrl** →.)

5. Move the cursor to Column B and make that one narrower. Leave about a half inch at the left of the numerals. (Don't make the column too narrow!)

6. Move the cursor to Cell D7 and press **F7** to exit from the table editor.

7. Press **Tab** once to add another row. Key **Totals** in Cell A8.

8. Save your table as **table.3**.

EXERCISE 9-3

One of the really nice features of tables is the spreadsheet capabilities. You need totals in all of the remaining cells. WordPerfect will do that for you automatically. All you have to do is tell WordPerfect how you would like the calculations performed.

Perform the calculations:

▶ **EXERCISE 9-4**

1. Move the cursor to Cell D3 and enter the table editor.

2. Choose **5 F**ormula. In the box for the formula, key **sum(b3:c3)** and press **Enter** twice. (Does that total look correct?)

3. With the cursor still in Cell D3, choose Move/Copy. In the little dialog box, choose Copy. Then choose **2 D**own. Key **5** in the *How Many?* slot and press **Enter** twice.

4. Move the cursor to Cell B8. Create a formula to add the numbers above the cell **(sum(b3:b7))** and check the numbers.

5. Copy the formula two times to the right and recalculate, if necessary.

6. Exit from the table editor and look at your document with Print Pre**v**iew. Then save it as **table.4** but keep it open.

N O T E

In some releases of the software, the amount will appear to be copied. You'll need to key **a** for Calculate to see the correct mid-year totals.

You've done very well with the table. But it's not finished yet. Some of the finishing touches are the most important when it comes to the appearance of a document.

Centering and changing lines:

▶ **EXERCISE 9-5**

1. Return to the table editor and choose **4 T**able. Choose **P**osition and set it at **C**enter. Close the Table Format dialog box. The table won't look any different than it did a moment ago.

2. Block all of Row 2 and choose **6 L**ines/Fill.

3. Choose **5 T**op and change the kind of lines at the top of the row to Double. Do the same with the **6 B**ottom of the cell.

4. Block all of Row 8. Choose **6 L**ines/Fill again. This time choose **F** for Fill. In the Fill Style and Color dialog box, choose **1** Fill St**y**le. Move the highlight to 10% and press **Enter** three times to return to the table editor.

5. Choose **6 L**ines/Fill again and choose **2** Border/Fill from the top of the dialog box. Choose **1 B**order style and change it to a Thick border. (This is for around the entire table.) Press **Enter** as many times as necessary to return to the table editor.

6. Move your cursor to Row 1. Choose **3 R**ow and change from Auto height to **3 F**ixed. Key **0.8** to make the cell nearly an inch high.

LESSON 9 WORDPERFECT TABLES 81

7. Go back to the **1 C**ell Format dialog box and choose **5 V**ertical Alignment. Choose **3 C**enter. This vertically centers the text in the space taken by the row. (It won't appear to be centered until you view your table with Print Pre**v**iew.)

8. Exit from the table editor. You may block the text of the title and change it to a large (perhaps 14 or 16 points) font, if you'd like.

9. Print your table. Then save it as **sales**. Keep it open on the screen.

MISCELLANEOUS TABLE FEATURES

You've barely scratched the surface of the things you can do with tables, but you're probably getting the picture. The next couple of pages will contain an assortment of table enhancements and features you might find useful. We'll use the **sales** table for some more practice.

Just as in a regular spreadsheet program, you can change a number in a WordPerfect table and recalculate. The totals will automatically reflect that change. You also can use other spreadsheet formulas.

EXERCISE 9-6

1. Phillipe wasn't resting. He was working hard in the first quarter. The $35 should have been $1,035. Move to Cell B4 and make that change.

2. Choose **T**able from the **L**ayout menu and then choose Calculate All. (You could have also returned to the table editor and recalculated. *Calculate All* works better in some versions of the software.)

3. Move your cursor to Cell D3 and return to the table editor. Use **Insert** to add another column BEFORE the cursor. When the change is made, your cursor will be in a new, empty Cell D3. We are going to average the sales for each salesperson.

4. Choose **F**ormula and key **ave(b3:c3)**. Return to the table editor. Copy that formula into the remaining cells in Column D and recalculate, if necessary. Do the averages appear to be correct?

5. Adjust the sizes of the columns that appear to be squashed and add shading to Cell D8. While you're in that cell, press **Backspace** to remove that total. Usually averages aren't totalled.

6. Close the table editor and key **Average** in Cell D2.

7. Print the document and save it as **sales.6** but keep it open.

If you'd like, you can remove all lines from the table, or you can remove lines from some of the cells. The procedure is much like when you added double lines to the column headings row. You also have to remove the border around the outside of the table. The border is separate from the lines. Also, you'll be surprised to find that the lines you inserted around the column headings won't be deleted with the rest of the lines. That's because they were set separately. If you want them removed, they will have to be deleted separately. When you finish, your table will look like Figure 9-6.

FIGURE 9-6
Table Without Lines

Salesperson	First	Second	Average	Mid-Year
Johnnie Jacks	$499.25	$540.00	$519.63	$1,039.25
Phillipe Darling	$1,035.89	$648.23	$842.06	$1,684.12
Yang Lin	$625.88	$569.12	$597.50	$1,195.00
Esther Flores	$385.90	$495.40	$440.65	$881.30
Diane Jones	$485.00	$1,146.50	$815.75	$1,631.50
Totals	$3,031.92	$3,399.25		$6,431.17

QUARTERLY AND MID-YEAR SALES EARNINGS

EXERCISE 9-7

1. Go into the table editor and block the entire table. Choose **6 L**ines/Fill and then **1 D**efault Line for the Entire Table.
2. Choose **1 L**ine Style and change the setting to None.
3. Return to the Table Lines dialog box and choose **2** Border/Fill and change the Border Style from Thick to None.
4. Return to your document. Preview it. It's pretty nice, isn't it?
5. Print the table and save it as **sales.7**.

FLOATING CELL

Another thing you can do is tie cells in the table to text in the document that contains the table. Let's key a short paragraph that includes references tied to cells in the table. Then we'll amend the table again and watch how the amounts in the paragraph change.

EXERCISE 9-8

1. Move your cursor to a double space below your table. Key the text illustrated in Figure 9-7. When you come to the ******, don't key the asterisks. Instead, follow these instructions:

   a. Press **Alt-F7** and choose **4 F**loating Cell and **1 C**reate.

   b. Choose **2 F**ormula and then press **F6** for Names. Then press **Enter** to choose Table_A. (This names the table in your document so it can be referenced by the floating cells.)

   c. Back in the Table Formula dialog box, *Table_A* should be showing. Immediately following the *A*, key a period and then the location for the desired information. In this case, the information is in Cell E8. Key **E8**.

   d. Press **Enter** twice to return to the Edit Floating Cell dialog box. Choose **3** Number **T**ype and then choose **5 C**urrency. Press **Enter** until you return to your document.

Open the Layout menu and choose Create **F**loating Cell.

LESSON 9 WORDPERFECT TABLES 83

2. Back in your text, the total should appear. Key the remainder of the paragraph.
3. At the *** notation, enter another floating cell that references Table_A. This time reference Cell D6.
4. Print your document and save it as **sales.8**. Keep it open.

> Here is a table illustrating our mid-year sales. Notice
> that the total sales are **. Esther is usually one of our
> better salespersons, and her average sales for this period
> have only been ***. Please double-check her quarter
> averages to see if an error was made.

FIGURE 9-7

Well, a check was run and indeed, Esther should have done better. She was ill part of the second quarter, but her first quarter sales should have been $885.90. We know how to fix that number in the table. Will it affect the reported average in the floating cell?

1. Position your cursor in Cell B6 and change the **3** to an **8**.
2. Open the **L**ayout menu and choose **T**ables. Then choose Calculate All.
3. Print your revised document. Then close it, saving it as **sales.9**.

▶ **EXERCISE 9-9**

Isn't this program incredible?

CONVERTING TABULATIONS

You can change a tabular document into a table. A short exercise will show you how easy it is.

1. Open **colors**. Block the entire document.
2. With the blocked tabular columns showing on the screen, press **Alt-F7** or choose **T**ables from the **L**ayout menu. Choose Create.
3. WordPerfect will ask about creating a table from Block. Choose **1 T**abular Text.
4. Look at your table. Close the table without saving.

▶ **EXERCISE 9-10**

IMPORTING SPREADSHEETS

If you work with a spreadsheet program, you can probably import a spreadsheet right into your WordPerfect document. Practice for that isn't included here, but you'll find that when you import a spreadsheet, it will come into WordPerfect as a table. Then you can manipulate it just like the **sales** table in this lesson.

JOINING TABLES

If you have a complicated table in which the columns are better if they aren't aligned vertically, you can create a second table immediately below the first table. When printed, the two tables will look like one large table, but you can have different combinations of columns.

A neat application of joined tables might be an organizational chart. Look at Figure 9-8. In this illustration, one [HRt] separates the two tables illustrated. If you leave out the hard return between them, the space will obviously be deleted. The black lines in this table show how you can join cells to carve out the parts of the table you want for the organizational chart. You'll join some cells and turn off lines around other cells until your chart looks just right. You may practice this on your own, if you'd like.

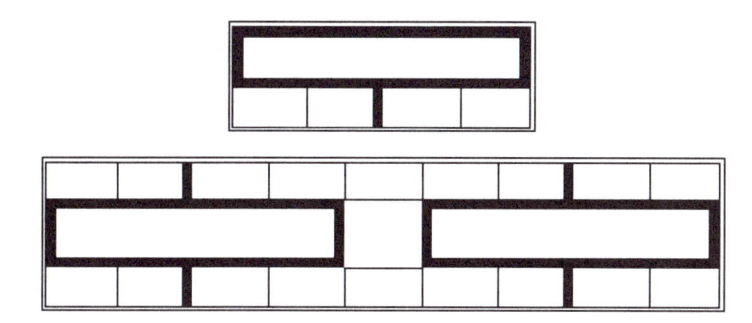

FIGURE 9-8
Beginning of an Organizational Chart

LANDSCAPE ORIENTATION

In all the work you've done so far in WordPerfect 6.0 for DOS, you've worked with the page in the normal *orientation*. The 8 1/2-inch edge is at the top and the 11-inch edge is at the side. This is referred to as the *portrait* orientation.

Sometimes you have a document or a table that is simply too wide to fit on the page, even when you change your margins to get a longer line length. For that reason and for other display purposes, it is sometimes necessary to turn the paper the other way. When the 11-inch edge is at the top and the 8 1/2-inch edge is at the side, it is said to be the landscape orientation. Some printers are unable to print in the *landscape* orientation. If WordPerfect will not allow you to make the choice, ask your instructor if you should skip this exercise.

The change from portrait to landscape is one of several choices you can make in the Paper Size/Type dialog box which is chosen from the Page Format dialog box. We'll learn about the Paper Size/Type command as we use it.

▶ **EXERCISE 9-11**

1. On a clear working screen, press **Shift-F8** and choose **3 P**age.
2. Choose **4** Paper **S**ize/Type and look at the sizes and shapes of pages available for your printer. As you move the highlight up and down the list, a description of the page appears in the lower right section of the dialog box.
3. Move the highlight to *Letter (Landscape)* and press **Enter** to choose it. Then press **Home, F7** to return to your document screen.
4. Prepare the table using the text illustrated in Figure 9-9. When you finish, print it and close it, saving it as trees.

Choose **P**age from the **L**ayout menu.

Aspen	Linden Basswood	Magnolia	Pomegranate	Sassafras
Oak	Catalpa	Silver Maple	Mesquite	Birch
Apple	Sunburst Locust	Mangrove	Prickly Ash	Blue Spruce
Horse Chestnut	Willow	Acacia	Red Maple	Grapefruit

▎**FIGURE 9-9**

▶ **SUMMARY**

This little lesson on tables should have given you a good idea of some of the ways you can use WordPerfect to help you with your work. The Tables feature is a powerful one. You've just tapped the possibilities.

Don't avoid tables. Look for ways to use the Tables feature in your work. It should save you much time and frustration.

LESSON 9 NOTES:

LESSON 10

Merge

OBJECTIVES

Upon completion of this lesson, you will be able to:

1. Create a form file and a data file.
2. Merge the form file with the data file.
3. Merge from the keyboard.

Estimated Time: 1 1/2 hours

While merge operations can be used for quite a variety of applications, WordPerfect's Merge feature is often used to combine lists of customers with standard documents, such as form letters. It's not absolutely imperative that you learn the terminology to use Merge and Sort. The terminology, however, helps you tie this WordPerfect feature to the same feature in other word processing programs.

Lesson 10 concentrates on the creation of form files and data files. In fact, you will learn a number of ways of preparing data files so you can choose the one that best fits your application. Finally you will learn to combine the form files and data files into a group of personalized documents. You'll be amazed to discover how powerful the Merge tool is in your WordPerfect program.

MERGE TERMINOLOGY

- **Merge Codes.** WordPerfect has dozens of codes that may be used for merges. They look a little strange when you put them into your documents because they are often two or more words run together.

- **Record.** A record is one complete entry in the data file. For example, if you have a list of names, addresses, and telephone numbers for a group of people, the complete information for one person is a record. An **ENDRECORD** code identifies the end of a record.

- **Field.** A field is one piece of data included in a record. There is no limit to the number of fields in a record. In some cases, the name might be broken into separate fields, or the city, state, and ZIP code might be considered separate fields so the list can be sorted more easily. Here are two different ways you might break up your data files:

Title	Name
First Name	Street Address
Last Name	City, State ZIP Code
Street Address	Telephone
City	
State	
ZIP Code	
Telephone	

    An **ENDFIELD** code marks the end of a field. It is always accompanied by a hard return. Both the ENDFIELD code and the hard return are inserted by pressing F9.

- **Form File.** This document is the shell or standard document. It contains text and codes that are combined with the data file—often a list of names and addresses.

- **Data File.** This is the list to be merged with the form file.

    Data files may be formatted in one of two ways—text data files, as illustrated in Figure 10-1, or table data files, as illustrated in Figure 10-2. In a text data file, the fields are in a vertical list, each ending with an ENDFIELD code which includes a hard return.

```
Johnny JumpupENDFIELD
333 Spring StreetENDFIELD
Coilton, WA 99034ENDFIELD
603-555-2334ENDFIELD
ENDRECORD
```

FIGURE 10-1
Text Data File

In a table data file, each field is in a table cell, and the data is displayed across the line of writing. If something doesn't fit on the line in a cell, it simply wraps to the next line.

Johnny Jumpup	333 Spring Street	Coilton, WA 99034	603-555-2334

FIGURE 10-2
Table Data File

CREATING A FORM FILE

Study Figure 10-4 and Figure 10-5. Figure 10-4 is a form file that can be merged with the data file in Figure 10-5 to produce several letters. The form file uses FIELD codes to request the appropriate information from the data file. In this particular letter, the telephone number in Field 4 isn't used, but you might want that information saved with the other information about the potential customer.

In the next two exercises, you will create a form file and then a data file. In real life, it doesn't matter which file is prepared first since you will save both and then merge them.

EXERCISE 10-1

1. Position the cursor at **Pos 4"**, 2 inches from the top of the page.

2. Press **Shift-F9** to open the Merge Codes dialog box and choose **1 F**orm to tell WordPerfect you are creating a form file.

3. The Merge Codes dialog box should open, looking much like Figure 10-3. Look at the list of merge codes at the left. These are some of the more common codes for form files.

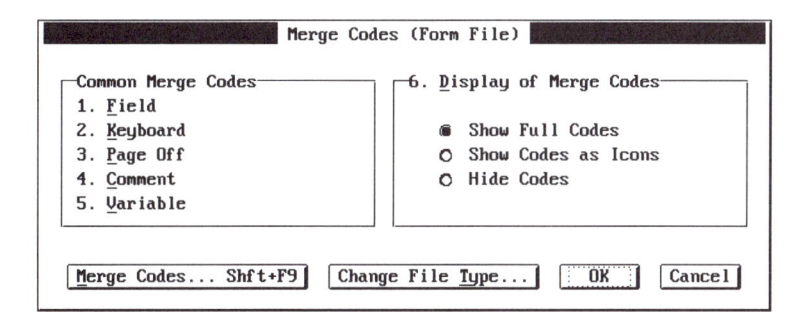

Open the **T**ools menu. Choose M**e**rge and then **D**efine. Then choose **1 F**orm.

```
┌─────────── Merge Codes (Form File) ───────────┐
│ ┌─Common Merge Codes─┐  ┌─6. Display of Merge Codes─┐
│ │ 1. Field           │  │  ● Show Full Codes         │
│ │ 2. Keyboard        │  │  ○ Show Codes as Icons     │
│ │ 3. Page Off        │  │  ○ Hide Codes              │
│ │ 4. Comment         │  │                            │
│ │ 5. Variable        │  │                            │
│ └────────────────────┘  └────────────────────────────┘
│                                                │
│ [Merge Codes... Shft+F9] [Change File Type...] [OK] [Cancel]
└────────────────────────────────────────────────┘
```

FIGURE 10-3
Merge Codes Dialog Box

4. Key **M** to choose the Merge Codes button. This opens an extended list of merge codes that are listed in alphabetic order. Key **D** which will take you directly to the DATE code. Press **Enter** to enter it into your document. Press **Enter** four times to quadruple space after the date.

5. Press **Shift-F9** to open the Merge Codes dialog box again and choose **1 F**ield. At the *Field* prompt, key **1** and press **Enter** to request the information in Field 1. (Field 1 contains the inside address.)

6. Press **Enter** twice to leave a double space. Key **Dear** and space once. Press **Shift-F9**, choose **F**ield, and key **2** to request Field 2. Press **Enter** once, key a colon, and double space. Your document should look like the top of Figure 10-4.

LESSON 10   MERGE   89

7. Retrieve **micro.ff** from the template disk, OR:

Key the remaining copy in Figure 10-4. Request Field 3 in the letter as shown. Close the letter, saving it as **micro.ff**. (This is a form file about micrographics).

FIGURE 10-4

```
                              DATE


FIELD(1)

Dear FIELD(2):

Thank you for your interest in imaging systems.  Image
Specialists is committed to imaging in the office.  We feel
that imaging helps businesses to improve their efficiency
and productivity.

In your letter, you mentioned FIELD(3) as the technology
you would like to research in your efforts to begin using
imaging in your office.  In response to that request, I am
enclosing several brochures on FIELD(3).

Please look through the brochures and get an idea of how
Image Specialists can serve you.  Then call me using the
special toll-free number listed on each of the brochures.
We can set up a time for a consultation to discuss the
procedure to follow in getting started with imaging.

Thank you for your interest in our company.  We are looking
forward to providing you with professionals who will analyze
your company's needs and recommend the best system for your
company.
                              Sincerely,


                              (your name)


(ref)

Enclosures
```

▶ CREATING A DATA FILE

Now we'll create the data file or list. You will see how easy it is to send a group of letters without keying each one individually.

TEXT DATA FILE

You learned earlier in this lesson that data files can be prepared in either *text* or *table* format. We'll begin with the text format. Study the names and address in Figures 10-5 and 10-6. See how they will fit with the field requests in the form file.

▶ **EXERCISE 10-2**

From the **T**ools menu, choose M**e**rge and then **D**efine.

1. Key the record in Figure 10-5. Press **F9** to insert the ENDFIELD codes as shown. (The hard returns are inserted automatically after ENDFIELD codes.)

2. At the end of the record, press **Shift-F9** for the Merge Codes dialog box.

3. Choose **2 D**ata Text. Choose **2 E**nd Record. (Now that you have identified the file as a data file, you can simply press **Shift-F9** and **2** or **E** to insert the ENDRECORD codes.)

▌**FIGURE 10-5**

```
Mr. Frank Weigel
Weigel Wire Works
453 Rummer Road
Brunswick, ME 00834ENDFIELD
Mr. WeigelENDFIELD
COM systemsENDFIELD
207-555-1200ENDFIELD
ENDRECORD
=============================
```

4. Retrieve **micro.df** from the template disk, OR:

Prepare the records in Figure 10-6 following the same procedure you used in Steps 1-3. Begin each new record on the line directly below the hard page break.

5. Check your work carefully. There must be the same number of fields in each record. Each field must contain the same information as the corresponding fields in other records.

6. Close the document, saving this list of prospective customers (the data file) as **micro.df**.

FIGURE 10-6

```
Mr. Berndt Helmke
Celle Engineering
6678 Celle Lane
Hamburg, VT 09221ENDFIELD
Mr. HelmkeENDFIELD
micrographicsENDFIELD
802-555-9866ENDFIELD
ENDRECORD
=============================
Ms. Dorothee Oppermann
Opperthee Sporting Goods
782 N. Kassel Street
Landeau, ME 00884ENDFIELD
Ms. OppermannENDFIELD
image printers and plottersENDFIELD
207-555-7639ENDFIELD
ENDRECORD
=============================
```

MERGING THE FILES

Once you have created the form and data files, it is a simple matter to merge them. We'll begin with a clear screen.

1. Press **Ctrl-F9** and choose **1** M**e**rge.

2. A prompt will ask for the name of the form file. Key **micro.ff** and press **Enter**. At the prompt for the data file, key **micro.df** and press **Enter**.

3. Press **Enter** again to start the merge or click the Merge button. At the bottom of the screen, WordPerfect reports the progress of the merge. Then your merged documents will appear on the screen. When the merge is complete, your cursor will be at the bottom of the final letter.

4. Use **Home,** ↑ to move backwards through your document a screenful at a time, and look at the merged letters. Check your letters with Print Pre**v**iew. Do they look good? If so, print the letters and close them, saving them as **micro-1.mrg**.

▶ **EXERCISE 10-3**

Open the **T**ools menu and choose **1** M**e**rge.

DATA FILES WITH NAMED FIELDS

In the merge you just completed, you worked with what are called *numbered fields*. In other words, the form file requested the information from the data file by number. Another way to prepare the form and data files is to name the fields. This is especially useful if if a record contains many fields. When working with named fields, WordPerfect prompts the next information to be entered. If you watch the prompts, you're less likely to skip information or get incorrect information in a field.

Normally you would make the decision to use named or numbered fields before beginning an application. However, to save time, we are going to go back to the form file and data file you just prepared and change them to merge documents with named fields.

▶ **EXERCISE 10-4**

1. Open **micro.ff**. Move the cursor to the *1* between the parentheses in the inside address. Delete the *1* and replace it with **customer**.

2. In the greeting, replace the *2* with **greeting**. In Paragraph 2, replace the *3* with **interest** (in both places).

3. Save the form file again, this time as **micro-n.ff** (form file with names), and close it.

4. Open **micro.df**. With the cursor at the top of the document, press **Shift-F9** and choose **3 F**ield **N**ames.

5. Key **customer** and press **Enter**. The field name will be entered in the box below. Key **greeting**, **interest**, and then **telephone**, each followed by pressing **Enter**. Press **F7** twice to close the dialog box.

6. Back in your document, the cursor is on the *M* of *Mr. Frank Weigel*. In the prompt position on the status line, WordPerfect is prompting that you are in the *customer* field. Move down through the list and see how the prompt changes for each field.

7. Move to the bottom of the list and add the customers listed in Figure 10-7. Keep an eye on the prompts as you work.

8. Save the remodeled data file as **micro-n.df** and close it.

▌**FIGURE 10-7**

```
Mr. Kim Lee
Lee Electronics
42 Center Street
Gainesville, NH 00912ENDFIELD
Mr. LeeENDFIELD
multimediaENDFIELD
603-555-9922ENDFIELD
ENDRECORD
===========================
Mr. Rudiger Phipps
Phipps Chipps
881 Overland Road
Brunswick, ME 00834ENDFIELD
Mr. PhippsENDFIELD
image printers and plottersENDFIELD
207-555-2244ENDFIELD
ENDRECORD
===========================
```

1. Merge **micro-n.ff** with **micro-n.df**.

2. Look through your documents. If everything looks OK, print only the letters to Mr. Lee and Mr. Phipps.

3. Close the document with the five letters, saving it as **micro-2.mrg**.

▶ **EXERCISE 10-5**

TABLE DATA FILES

As you learned earlier, there are two ways to prepare data files. You can key the data files with the information in a list down the left side of the screen as you have prepared the text data files so far in this lesson, or you can key the data into a table. Let's prepare a table data file to be merged with the well-used form file you prepared in the first exercise.

1. Press **Shift-F9** and choose **3** Data **T**able. Then choose **1** Create a Table with Field **N**ames.

2. Key **customer** and press **Enter**. Then repeat the procedure for **greeting**, **interest**, and **telephone**. Finally, press **F7** twice. The cursor will be in the cell for Mr. Weigel's name and address.

3. Key the name and address of the first potential customer in Figure 10-5 into the first cell of the table. Let the text wrap around as the cell is filled until you come to what should be the end of a line (after the name *Weigel*). Then press **Enter**.

4. **Tab** to the second column and key the greeting for Mr. Weigel. **Tab** to the third column for the area of interest and the fourth column for the phone. When you finish with the first record, your table should look like Figure 10-8.

▶ **EXERCISE 10-6**

customer	greeting	interest	telephone
Mr. Frank Weigel Weigel Wire Works 453 Rummer Road Brunswick, ME 00834	Mr. Weigel	COM system	207-555-1200

FIGURE 10-8
Table Data File Record

5. Press **Tab** again and key Mr. Helmke's name and address. Continue until the information for all three customers has been keyed.

6. Save the table data file as **mic-tab.df** and close it.

7. Merge **micro.ff** with **mic-tab.df** and look over the results. The letters should look just like the letters in your first merge. Close the document without saving it.

KEYBOARD MERGE

When you wish to personalize only one or two letters, it isn't efficient to prepare a data file to be merged with the form file. A better way is to do what's called a *keyboard merge*. With this procedure, you first prepare the form file. Then you enter the variable information during the merge.

This kind of merge uses a **KEYBOARD** merge code that causes the merge to stop for you to key the appropriate information. Let's learn as we do a simple keyboard merge exercise.

▶ **EXERCISE 10-7**

1. Key the paragraph in Figure 10-9. At the location for the first KEYBOARD code, press **Shift-F9**, choose **1 F**orm, and then **2 K**eyboard.

2. In the Parameter Enter dialog box, key **patient name** as the prompt for the first variable. Press **Enter** to insert the code and the variable into your document. The variable information in the figure is shaded. On your screen it will appear to be normal text.

3. Continue keying the document until you come to the next KEYBOARD code. Press **Shift-F9** and key **K**. Key **He/She** for the variable. Continue in this way until you finish the document.

4. When you finish, close the document, saving it as **refer.ff**.

Open the **T**ools menu. Choose M**e**rge, **D**efine, and then **1 F**orm. Choose **2 K**eyboard.

FIGURE 10-9

```
This is a referral of KEYBOARD(patient name) to your care.
KEYBOARD(He/She) lives at KEYBOARD(address).
KEYBOARD(patient name) is a KEYBOARD(male/female) who is
KEYBOARD(age) years old. KEYBOARD(He/She) has a blood
pressure of KEYBOARD(blood pressure) and is suffering from
KEYBOARD(symptoms).  A complete medical chart is available
upon request.
```

▶ **EXERCISE 10-8**

1. The patient information is illustrated in Figure 10-10. To merge the form document with that information, begin with a clear screen. Press **Ctrl-F9** and choose **1 M**erge.

2. At the prompt for the form file, key **refer.ff** and press **Enter**. Press **Enter** again to begin the merge. (You don't have a data file for this merge.)

3. Part of the form file will appear on the screen with the cursor at the location of the first variable. Look in the lower left corner of the screen. You are being prompted to enter the patient name. Key **Isabella Legg** and press **F9** to move the cursor to the next "blank."

4. Continue moving through the document, following the prompts to fill in the information about Ms. Legg and pressing **F9** after each piece of information.

Choose M**e**rge and then **R**un from the **T**ools menu.

5. After keying Ms. Legg's "symptoms," press **F9** to add the final sentence. This also ends the merge. Check over your work. If everything is correct, print the referral and close it, saving it as **refer.leg**.

6. Repeat Steps 1-5 for Mr. Hartmann. When you finish, print his referral and close it, this time saving it as **refer.har**.

FIGURE 10-10

```
Patient 1                        Patient 2
Isabella Legg                    Harley Hartmann
333 Erie Street                  77 Yoman Court
Epsonville, IA 49876             Yaleston, IA 49879
Female                           Male
Age:  33                         Age:  77
Blood Pressure:  98/58           Blood Pressure:  180/95
Symptoms: dizziness              Symptoms:  chest pains
                                   and shortness of breath
```

Keyboard merges can be very useful. For example, you could set up a memo form in keyboard merge format. Then each time you needed to create a memo, you would choose Merge and use F9 to move from one KEYBOARD code to another.

▶ SUMMARY

This lesson has been a quick introduction to the marvelous magic of Merge. It gets even better, as you'll learn in Lesson 11. You were presented with some options—whether to prepare your data files as text or table files and how to break down the record into fields that work well for your particular application.

You also have the choice of using named or numbered fields in your merges. Numbered fields are fine for many applications. Where the named fields become so critically important is when you are working with data files that contain many fields or when the information to be entered isn't in a neat little list. In those cases you'll find the field name prompts extremely useful.

LESSON 10 NOTES:

ACTIVITY

LESSON 9 & 10 ACTIVITIES

LESSON 9

1. What are the names for the vertical parts of a table, the horizontal parts of a table, and the place where the vertical part meets the horizontal part?

2. Why don't you have to worry about having the correct number of rows and columns for your tables when you create the table?

3. What must you do in the table editor if you wish to apply the same formatting to a number of table cells?

4. What is the number type choice when you are working with figures that represent dollars and cents?

5. What other kind of computer software does a WordPerfect table resemble?

6. What formula would you use if you wished to add the figures in cells C2, C3, C4, C5, and C6?

7. What is the name of the feature that enables you to put a figure from the table into the surrounding text, and the figure will update when changes are made to the table?

8. What is the orientation when paper is used sideways—with the long edge at the top? What is it called with the short edge at the top?

ACTIVITY

LESSON 10

1. What kind of merge file contains the shell document or standard text?

2. What kind of merge file contains the list or the names and addresses (in the case of a mailing)?

3. What part of the "list" contains the complete information about any person or product?

4. When checking over your data file after preparing it, you must check to be certain that each record has the same number of something. What is that something?

5. When you put an ENDFIELD code into your document, WordPerfect automatically enters another code. What is it? What two codes are entered when you put an ENDRECORD code into your document?

6. What kind of merge uses only a form file, and you enter the variable information while the merge is running?

Reference Questions. Turn in the *WordPerfect Reference* to the BIG section on Merge. Near the beginning of the section, information is given about Data Files and an illustration shows a screen containing four records. Into how many fields is each person's name and address broken? What are those fields?

The information beside the illustration tells you how many fields you may have in each record. What is that number?

100 ACTIVITY

LESSON 11

Handling Correspondence

OBJECTIVES

Upon completion of this lesson, you will be able to:

1. Create envelopes for single letters.
2. Create envelopes in merge applications.
3. Work with Merge data options.
4. Create labels for your mailings.
5. Sort your data files.

Estimated Time: 1 1/2 hours

You've learned to create a variety of documents. Now you will learn ways to deliver these documents. You could, of course, send them electronically through a modem to someone who also has access to a network. More often, however, the documents are sent by mail and need to be addressed. In this lesson we'll learn how easy it is to prepare envelopes and labels.

What you can do with envelopes and labels depends on your printer. WordPerfect knows from the printer you have selected what kinds of forms you can print. Most laser printers, for example, have an apparatus near the paper tray to feed single envelopes. If you print envelopes for this training, you can print on paper folded in half lengthwise, or you can cut paper to the exact size of the usual #10 business envelope (4.13" x 9.5").

SINGLE ENVELOPES

WordPerfect helps you prepare envelopes for single letters. You prepared a letter called **furnture** in a review exercise at the end of Lesson 5. Let's prepare an envelope for that letter.

1. Open **furnture**. Press **Alt-F12**.

2. Look at the Envelope dialog box. Notice that WordPerfect has already lifted the inside address from the letter and placed it in the mailing address box.

3. Choose **4 R**eturn Address and key your own name and address. You shouldn't use it in the classroom, but look at the choice just above **R**eturn Address. You can tell WordPerfect to remember your name and address so you don't have to key it every time you prepare an envelope. (DO NOT make that selection.)

4. Choose **6** POSTNET **B**ar Code and key the nine-digit ZIP code in the address. (Any printer that prints graphically can add the bar code to your envelope.)

5. Press **Enter** until you are returned to your document. The envelope will be on page 2 following the letter. Print only the envelope. Your printer may prompt you to feed the envelope when WordPerfect sends an envelope print command to the printer.

6. Close the document without saving.

> **EXERCISE 11-1**
>
> Choose **E**nvelope from the **L**ayout menu.

MERGED ENVELOPES

That was easy, wasn't it? Preparing envelopes for letters prepared in a merge application is nearly as easy. This is done as part of the merge. We'll merge your form and data files again and learn to make envelopes along with the letters.

1. Go to the Run Merge dialog box. Key **micro.ff** for the form file and **micro.df** for the data file. Then choose Da**t**a File Options.

2. This dialog box has quite a lot of very useful options. We'll look at some of them shortly. For now we're interested in Envelopes, and that choice is on the lower right side of the box. Choose **E**nvelopes.

3. In order for this merge to prepare the envelopes, you must request the field(s) containing the inside address. Choose **5 M**ailing Address and press **Shift-F9**.

> **EXERCISE 11-2**

4. Choose **1 F**ield. At the *Field* prompt, press **1** and then **Enter**. Press **F7** to exit that portion of the dialog box. Look at the rest of this dialog box. Note that you can include a return address here also.

5. Choose OK and then choose M**e**rge. The cursor will again be at the bottom of the merged letters, and the envelopes will follow the letters. Look at your envelopes.

6. Print one envelope and close the document without saving it.

> **NOTE**
>
> In this case, we can't include the POSTNET bar code because the ZIP code number is buried in the address. If you wanted to include the POSTNET bar code on the envelopes prepared in a merge, the data file would have to be prepared with the ZIP code number in a field by itself.

That was pretty easy, too. As you noticed, providing a way for you to create envelopes is only one of the options available in the Data File Options dialog box. Let's return to the dialog box and discuss some of the other options. Pay attention to what you learn. The features won't be practiced until the review exercises at the end of the lesson.

▶ **EXERCISE 11-3**

1. Return to the Run Merge dialog box. The Data File Options portion will probably still be displayed. It should look like Figure 11-1.

2. Find each of the features in the box as they are discussed in the paragraphs below. When you finish, choose Cancel to close the box without merging again.

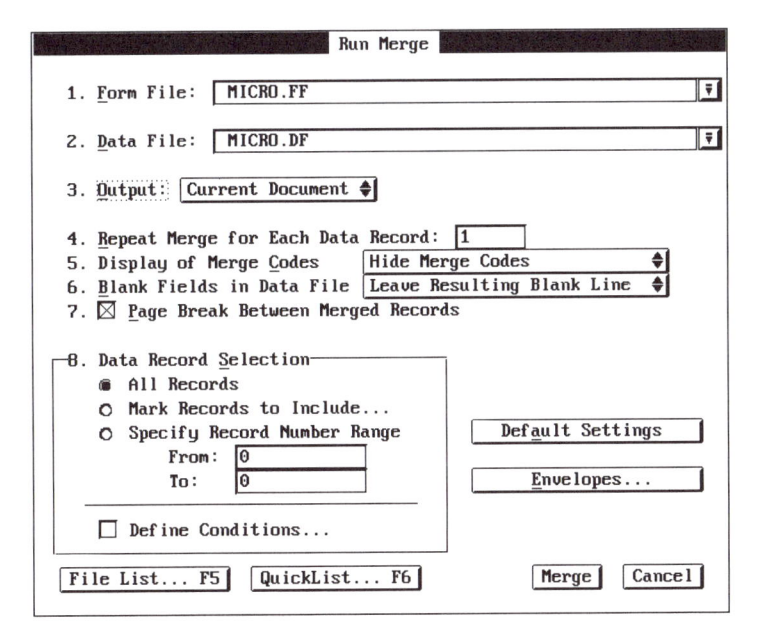

FIGURE 11-1
Extended Run Merge Dialog Box

```
                    Run Merge
1. Form File:  [MICRO.FF                    ]
2. Data File:  [MICRO.DF                    ]
3. Output: [Current Document ▲▼]

4. Repeat Merge for Each Data Record: [1]
5. Display of Merge Codes     [Hide Merge Codes      ▲▼]
6. Blank Fields in Data File  [Leave Resulting Blank Line ▲▼]
7. ☒ Page Break Between Merged Records

┌8. Data Record Selection─────────────────────┐
│   ● All Records                             │
│   ○ Mark Records to Include...              │
│   ○ Specify Record Number Range   [Default Settings] │
│         From: [0]                           │
│         To:   [0]                           │
│                                   [Envelopes...]    │
│                                             │
│   ☐ Define Conditions...                    │
└─────────────────────────────────────────────┘
[File List... F5]  [QuickList... F6]    [Merge] [Cancel]
```

- **O**utput. Normally the results of a merge will go to a clear screen. After all, you have nine screens from which to choose! But you can change it so the Output will be into the same document you currently have open.

- **R**epeat Merge. You can also have WordPerfect prepare more than one document for each record in the list. This would be great if you were preparing labels for a mailing, and you needed duplicate labels—one for the outside of the envelope and one for the form letter inside.

- **B**lank Fields. This item is for situations where information might be missing in a record. If you have a company name field in your data file and there is no company name, a blank line will be left during the merge unless you change this option.

- **P**age Breaks are usually between merged records. For example, when you merged your letters, each ended up on a separate page. If you wished to merge the names and addresses into a list, however, you wouldn't want each customer on a separate page. Then you need to deselect this option before merging.

- Data Record **S**election allows you to send letters to only some of the people in your list. You can choose the first portion of the list, the last portion of the list, or you can go through and mark those records you'd like included. This is a good way to prepare only bills for customers whose accounts are more than two months overdue or who owe more than $500, for example.

As you work with Merge, explore this dialog box more thoroughly. You'll find that it enables you to do just about anything you want with your merge.

▸ LABELS

Whenever you wish to prepare a document on something other than the standard paper size, you must include a special code in your document to tell WordPerfect you've changed the paper size or type. Up to now you've used the standard paper size for everything you've done except the wide table at the end of Lesson 9. For the table, you used landscape orientation. Envelopes use landscape orientation, too, but the settings are taken care of by WordPerfect.

WordPerfect has made the preparation of labels easy, but a Labels code must be inserted into your document. There are many sizes and styles of labels. Go to the Page Format dialog box now and choose **5 L**abels to look at the list.

As you can see, the list of labels includes the brand name and the label style. Beneath the list is a description of the details of the label size and the paper size. The options in the lower right corner allow you to look at labels for laser printers only, for tractor-fed (pin-fed) printers only, or for both. (The default is to display both.)

One of the most popular label sizes is 3" x 10" labels on a full sheet of paper. These labels are usually set up as part of a merge. The procedure is to create a form file, complete with Paper Size/Type code, include the appropriate Field codes, and then merge the form file with the data file. Before we merge, though, let's practice.

104   LESSON 11   HANDLING CORRESPONDENCE

EXERCISE 11-4

1. Move your highlight to the *3M 7730* labels. That choice is near the top of the list.

2. Press **Enter** to select that label description. Look briefly at the dialog box that appears and then press **Enter** again. The paper should appear to be very narrow.

3. Each label is considered a logical page, so the address on one label is separated from the address on the next label by a hard page break. With that in mind, you can key the addresses for the labels and separate them manually.

4. Key your own name and address. Press **Ctrl-Enter** for a hard page break and key the name and address of a friend. Add another hard page break.

5. Retrieve **names** from the template disk, OR:

Continue keying addresses, separated by hard page breaks, until you have 10 or 11 addresses.

6. Go to Print Pre**v**iew to see how the names and addresses will look when printed. The document should look much like the portion of a page illustrated in Figure 11-2. If possible, print your labels. Then close the document, saving it as **labels**.

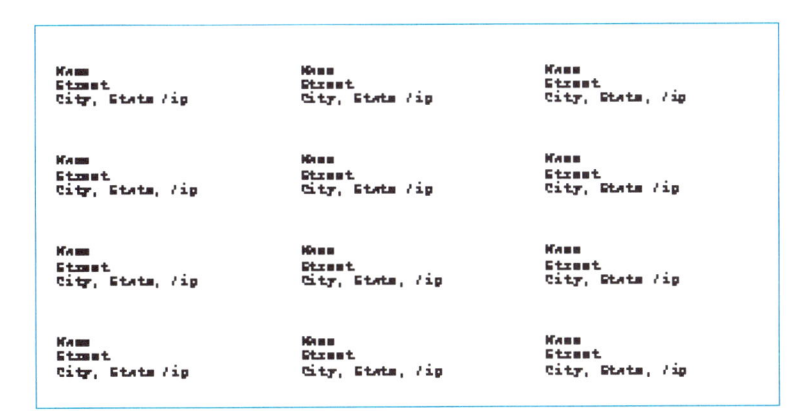

FIGURE 11-2
Labels

DOCUMENT INITIAL CODES

When you create the form file for labels to be printed on a laser printer, you must put the Paper Size/Type code in a location that causes it to affect the entire document. The choice for that location is found in the Document Format dialog box. It is called Document Initial Codes.

Your list is too small for you to appreciate how the labels will work. We will increase the size of the list. Then we'll create the label form and merge the list with the label form. Read all of the instructions for the next two exercises before beginning. Then follow along carefully so that your merge is successful.

EXERCISE 11-5

1. To prepare the data file, open **micro.df**. Reveal your codes so you can see as you position the cursor at the top of the document, above all codes except the [OpenStyle:InitialCodes] code. Turn on Block.

2. Press **Home**, **Home**, ↓ to extend the block to the bottom of the document.

3. Press **Ctrl-c** to copy the block. Then press **Ctrl-v** to paste the block at the bottom of the list.

4. Press **Home, Home**, ↓ to move the cursor to the bottom of the list again and press **Ctrl-v** again. Repeat this step one more time. You should now have 12 names in your list.

5. Close the document, saving it as **mic-big.df**.

EXERCISE 11-6

1. To prepare the form file, press **Shift-F8,** choose **4 D**ocument, and then **1** Document Initial **C**odes.

2. A special window should open, waiting for your codes. Press **Shift-F8** and choose **P**age and then **L**abels to open the Labels dialog box.

3. Move the highlight to the *3M 7730* label definition and press **Enter**.

4. Choose **3** Center **P**ages and press **Enter** twice. You should still be on the Document Initial Codes screen, and three codes should be there: [Labels Form], [Paper Sz/Typ], and [Cntr Pgs:On]. Press **F7** and then **Home**, **F7** to return to your working screen.

5. Open the Merge Codes dialog box. Choose **1 F**orm File and request **F**ield **1**.

6. Save your labels form as **lab-30.ff** (30 labels per page) and close it.

7. Merge **lab-30.ff** with **mic-big.df**. Look at the labels that result. Check them in Print Pre**v**iew. Print your labels, if you can.

8. Save the document as **lab-30.mrg** and close it.

1. Open the **L**ayout menu and then choose **D**ocument and Document Initial **C**odes.

2. Open the **L**ayout menu and then choose **P**age and **L**abels.

That was pretty easy, wasn't it? If you'd like, you can print hundreds of labels this way. To review:

1. Choose the label size/type. If you are merging, put the code for the labels and a Center Pages code (to center the address on the label, regardless of the number of lines) in your Document Initial Codes.

2. Combine the label form with a data file and print the labels.

Out of the large list of labels that are available, you should be able to find a size that matches your needs. Before deciding which label to use, visit an office supply store and look at the variety of labels you can buy—labels that come on individual sheets or continuous-feed labels depending, of course, on the kind of printer you are using. If you choose to prepare labels using a laser printer, be sure to buy laser printer labels, because they are manufactured to withstand the heat that's applied to documents as they are printed in a laser printer.

SORT

The records in your data file may be sorted prior to merging them with the form file. For example, if you are preparing a bulk mailing, it would be highly desirable to have the names and addresses sorted by ZIP code to save hand sorting after the documents are prepared. In other situations, it might be preferable to arrange the items alphabetically.

Let's learn as we practice.

EXERCISE 11-7a

1. Open **micro-n.df**. This is the data file with the named fields.
2. Press **Ctrl-F9** and choose **2 S**ort. Press **Enter** to bypass the Source and Destination dialog box.
3. The Sort dialog box will appear. At the top, you can see that WordPerfect figured out that this is a Merge Sort. (We'll look at the other types later.) Let's learn how to sort.

To set up this sort, we must set *keys*. The keys tell WordPerfect how you'd like the list sorted and how to identify the location of the criteria on which you are sorting. The first criteria on which we'll sort is ZIP code.

The ZIP code is the **last** word in the **last** line of the first field in each record. You can't count it as the third word on the line because some cities have two or more words in their names, such as New York. You can't count the line containing the city, state, and ZIP code as the fourth line of the address because, in some cases, an address might have three or five lines.

In a WordPerfect Sort, you indicate the **last** of something with **-1**. So the ZIP code in these addresses is in the Field 1, Line -1, and Word -1.

The *type* refers to whether the sort is Alphabetic or Numeric. Numeric includes only those numerals that vary in size. So ZIP code numbers, telephone numbers, and Social Security numbers use Alphabetic sort.

Ord refers to order. The up arrow indicates that the records will be sorted in an ascending order—in other words, the numbers will get larger. Sometimes you might want to sort from larger to smaller, so you would change to a down arrow.

LESSON 11 HANDLING CORRESPONDENCE 107

Now that you know all the tough stuff, let's get back to the exercise.

▶ **EXERCISE 11-7b**

1. Choose **2** Sort **K**eys to move the cursor into the Keys portion of the dialog box. Then choose **2 E**dit. The Edit Sort Keys dialog box will appear, looking much like Figure 11-3.

   | **FIGURE 11-3**
   | Edit Sort Keys Dialog Box

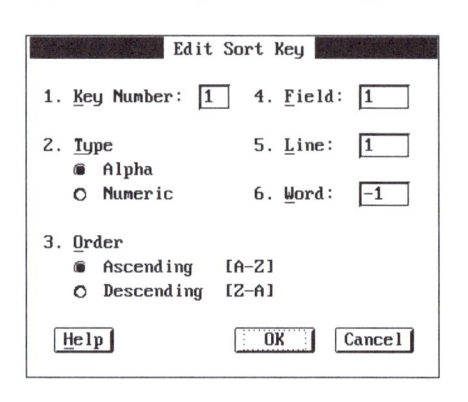

   ```
   ┌─────── Edit Sort Key ───────┐
   │ 1. Key Number: [1]  4. Field: [1]   │
   │                                     │
   │ 2. Type          5. Line:  [1]      │
   │    ● Alpha                          │
   │    ○ Numeric     6. Word:  [-1]     │
   │                                     │
   │ 3. Order                            │
   │    ● Ascending  [A-Z]               │
   │    ○ Descending [Z-A]               │
   │                                     │
   │  [Help]        [ OK ]  [Cancel]     │
   └─────────────────────────────────────┘
   ```

2. Change **5 L**ine to **-1** and **6 W**ord to **-1**. Choose OK and then press **F7** to get out of the Keys portion of the dialog box.

3. Press **Enter** to Perform the Action.

4. Look through the list. Are the potential customers in ZIP code order? Save the document with the same name. Keep it open on the screen.

Mr. Phipps and Mr. Weigel have the same ZIP code. It is only by accident that they are in alphabetic order. Let's go back and set it up so that they are always in the correct order. We will do this by adding a second Sort criteria. WordPerfect will sort first by ZIP code and then by last name. The last names of the potential customers are the last word in the first line of the first field.

▶ **EXERCISE 11-8**

1. For the sake of practice, go through the list and change the ZIP code numbers so that all of them are 00834. Then return to the Sort dialog box.

2. Choose **2** Sort **K**eys. Then choose **1 A**dd. The Edit Sort Keys dialog box will appear, and the first item in the dialog box will tell you that you are now working with Key 2.

3. Set Key 2 so that it will sort on Field 1, Line 1, and Word -1. Then choose OK and **F7** to exit from the Keys portion of the dialog box.

4. Press **Enter** to start the sort. Your potential customers should all be in alphabetic order, now.

5. Close the document without saving it.

108   LESSON 11   HANDLING CORRESPONDENCE

THINK a little about what you did here. If you wanted a list that was completely alphabetized, you'd set it up so Key 1 looked at last names. You could set Key 2 to look at first names, if you'd like, so all of the Smiths or Andersons could be alphabetized. In situations where people have "compound" names, like La Rue or Vanden Boogaard, you must use hard spaces. Remember how to key a hard space? It's *Home, Space* and it ties the words together as one word.

LINE SORT

Let's look at a different kind of sort. Line Sort is used when the text you want sorted is in fields or columns across the page. You can use this for a variety of different applications. You are still working with fields and setting the keys for sorting. We'll begin by creating a text file.

▶ **EXERCISE 11-9**

1. Clear all tabs. Set a **L**eft tab at **+2.5"** and a **D**ecimal tab at **+6"**.

2. Retrieve **linesort.1** from the template disk, OR:

Key the columns illustrated in Figure 11-4. Save the document as **linesort.1**. Keep it open on the screen.

Carol Anderson	Stevens Point, WI 54481	455.00
Walter Anderson	Phoenix, AZ 88471	998.00
Betty Boneske	Oshkosh, WI 54901	334.00
Judy Anne Boneske	Menasha, WI 54952	110.00
Pedro De Pino	Butternut, WI 54914	15.00
Carol Morgan	Wisconsin Dells, WI 53965	24.00
Dale R. Nelson	Butte des Morts, WI 54927	1290.00
Elizabeth Reichert	Milwaukee, WI 53211	1199.00
Alberta Weigel	Hendersonville, NC 28739	786.00
Earl Wiesmann	Ladysmith, WI 54848	3.00

▶ **FIGURE 11-4**

3. Go to the Sort dialog box. Set Key 1 so the list is sorted by *city*. Perform the Sort. (Did you set Key 1 at Field 2, Word 1?)

4. Return to the Sort dialog box and change it so the list is sorted by ZIP code number. (Set Key 1 at Field 2, Word -1.)

5. Sort the list by last names. You may use *-1* if your software works, otherwise join the middle names or initials to the first name with a hard space so you can sort on Word 2.)

6. Sort by amount due (Field 3). This is your first **Num**eric Sort. Sort the list first in Ascending order. Then sort it again in Descending order.

N O T E

IMPORTANT: In the 6.0a interim release of the software (dated 9-13-93) any Line Sort that uses *-1* doesn't work. To sort this list of cities by ZIP code, you would have to put hard spaces in the city names made up of more than one word. Then set up the sort so that you are sorting on Word 3.

As you can see, Sort is quite flexible. It can also sort paragraph material and tables. With Paragraph Sort, each paragraph is considered a field, and paragraphs are separated by two hard returns. In tables, the rows will be sorted, much like Line Sort. If you don't want the rows containing headings to be sorted along with the rest of the table, you must block the table rows to be sorted before opening the Sort dialog box.

▶ SELECT

You can use Select to separate out specific records, providing they have some commonality. In the list showing on your screen, set Key 1 so it points to the field where the select criteria is located. Then set up the Select formula and perform the action. Let's try it.

▶ **EXERCISE 11-10**

1. Return to the Sort dialog box. If it isn't already set, set Key 1 at Field 3, Word 1. Then choose **3 S**elect Records.

2. Key the following formula: **key1=>900**. Perform the action. WordPerfect separates out the three people with the large bills and deletes the remaining people from the list.

3. Close the list without saving. You may want the entire list to practice with Sort and Select on your own.

▶ SUMMARY

In this lesson you prepared the text for envelopes and labels to go with documents to be mailed. If your printer has the capability, this procedure isn't especially difficult. You also learned how to re-arrange your lists before they are sent to the printer using the Sort feature. Sort can be used for many things. A simple Alphabetic Sort of a quick list of anything is useful.

LESSON 11 NOTES:

REVIEW

EXERCISE 1

Clear all tabs and set one tab at **5"**. Return to the document screen and prepare a form file as illustrated in Figure 11-5. Save the file as **image.ff**.

FIGURE 11-5

```
FIELD(1)                                    FIELD(4)
```

Merge **image.ff** with **micro-n.df**. In the Data Options section of the Merge dialog box, deselect **7 P**age Break Between Merged Records. You should end up with a list of the five customers that you worked with in Lesson 10. Had you not deselected the page break option, all five customers would have been on separate pages.

Print your merged list. Then close it, saving it as **image.mrg**.

EXERCISE 2

Set up a text data file with named fields. The field names are listed in the order in which your boss would like them in Figure 11-6.

FIGURE 11-6

```
account number;first name;middle initial;last name;company
name;street;city;state;zip;phone;amount due
```

Figure 11-7 lists ten customers, their company names, their account numbers, telephone numbers, and amounts due. Some of the information is missing. Remember that an ENDFIELD code must mark the place for the missing information. Key the information for the first two customers in the data file.

Retrieve **bloom** from the template disk, OR:

Key the data for the remaining eight customers. Since the data is out of order, keeping an eye on the prompt in the lower left corner of the screen as you key should help you get all of the information into the correct fields.

When you finish, save the data file as **bloom.df** but keep it open.

REVIEW

FIGURE 11-7

```
Iris Inge                        #8611
Irish Creation                   $117.98
987 Ibsen Street
Indianapolis, ID 83634           317-555-9075

Rose R. Ramirez                  #1496
Runner's Rags                    $41.50
6789 Robin Lane
Rockton, RI 02954                401-555-8931

Petunia P. Peterson              #4821
Petunias & Petals                $992.57
543 Park Place, S.W.
Perryville, TX 76682             214-555-1956

Lily L. Larsen                   #6223
1213 Lanskron Lane               $763.64
Lexington, IL 61764

Pearl Poppy                      #5488
Puppies and Pets                 $125.90
6732 Polk Street
Pittsburgh, WI 54461             715-555-4453

Mari Gold                        #8821
Mari's Menagerie                 $34.79
231-A Garden Street
Gardena, ME 04940                207-555-7782

Gary G. Gardenia                 #2301
Gardenia Gardens                 $1,056.24
143 Gingham
Gillingham, TX 75921             806-555-5561

Bill B. Bloom                    #4439
543 Bixby Street                 $789.56
Bloomington, OK 74562            405-555-9975

Daisy D. Ditson                  #2399
Dixie's Dilemma                  $5.39
7632 Ann Street
Dixonville, DE 19811             302-555-1490

Betty Blum                       #3296
Buttons and Balloons             $126.98
657 Johnson Drive
Jackson, MN 56143                218-555-8225
```

REVIEW

a. Sort the customers by ZIP code. Save the sorted list as **bloom-a.df** and close it. Set tabs and prepare a form file to prepare a list of customers. Include the customer's last name at the left margin, the city, state, and ZIP code at **+2"**, and the amount due at a **D**ecimal tab set at **+6"**. Save the form file as **bloom-a.ff**. Merge and print the list and close it, saving it as **bloom-a.lst**.

b. Sort the customers by amount due, in descending order. Save the sorted list as **bloom-b.df** and close it. Use Merge to combine the reorganized list with the same form file you used for the exercise above. Print the new list and close it, saving it as **bloom-b.lst**.

c. Sort the list by account number, in ascending order. Save the sorted list as **bloom-c.df** and close it. Replace information in the middle column with the account numbers. Adjust the columns so the document is more attractive. Merge and print again, and close the document, saving it as **bloom-c.lst**.

d. Open **lab-30.ff** and revise it so it looks like Figure 11-8. The special codes prevent you from having too much space between the first name and last name when the customers have no middle initial. The dots between items show where you should put spaces.

Because your label is so narrow, the FIELD codes on the first line and the second line will wrap. That's OK. Put the hard returns in place where they should be. The IFNOTBLANK and ENDIF codes may be chosen from the Merge Codes list that appears when you choose the **M**erge Codes button at the bottom of the Merge Codes (Form File) dialog box. Save the form file as **bloom-d.ff**.

```
FIELD(2)•IFNOTBLANK(3)FIELD(3)•ENDIF FIELD(4)
FIELD(5)
FIELD(6)
FIELD(7),•FIELD(8)•FIELD(9)
```

FIGURE 11-8

Merge **bloom-d.ff** with **bloom-a.df**. Before merging, remember to choose the option in the Data Options that eliminates the blank line on the labels of customers for which you have no company name. Print the labels on plain paper and close the document. Save the document as **bloom-d.lst**.

LESSON 12

Multiple-Page Documents

OBJECTIVES

Upon completion of this lesson, you will be able to:

1. Use headers and footers.
2. Use automatic page numbering.
3. Use footnotes and endnotes.
4. Control page endings.

Estimated Time: 1/2 hour

Most of the documents you've created so far have been short enough that they fit onto one page. In real life, documents are much longer than that. Special formatting is needed for multiple-page documents so that the reader doesn't get the pages mixed up.

Headers, footers, and page numbering are all helpful to the reader of longer documents. You'll also find, as you complete the exercises in this lesson, that it is easy to give your longer documents continuity with these formatting tools.

HEADERS AND FOOTERS

Headers and footers are used to tie a document together. They may be used to identify the page, the chapter, or the document. We'll begin by adding a header to a short document you've already created.

> **EXERCISE 12-1**
>
> Choose **H**eader/Footer/Watermark from the **L**ayout menu.

1. Open **gifts.4r2**. Press **Shift-F8** to open the Format dialog box. Choose **5 H**eader/Footer/Watermark.

2. Look at the dialog box. From this box, you can create two headers, two footers, and/or two watermarks for your document. (We'll reserve the use of watermarks for a later lesson.)

3. Choose **1 H**eader and then **1** Header **A**. In the little dialog box that opens, press **Enter** to choose **1 A**ll pages. Your document will seem to disappear, and the status line at the bottom of the screen will report that you are on the Header A screen.

4. Key **International Giftgiving** (not in bold). Give the command for Flush Right, key the word **Page**, space once, and press **Ctrl-p**. A *1* will appear. That's your page number. Look at the codes. WordPerfect has really inserted a page number CODE.

5. Press **F7** or click the *Press F7* command at the bottom of the screen. Either will return you to your document.

6. Look at your document in Print Pre**v**iew. Return to your document screen and change to the Page mode. The header should show in both places.

7. In the Page mode, point to the header with the mouse pointer and double click. You will be returned to the special screen where you created the header.

8. Change *Giftgiving* to two words, each with a capital *G* at the beginning. Follow either method in Step 5 to return to your document.

9. Print the document. Then close it, saving it as **gifts.hed**.

Creating and editing that header was pretty easy, wasn't it? What's more, the results are gratifying. Footers work the same way. Here are some miscellaneous new and review facts about headers and footers:

- As you noticed in the Header/Footer/Watermark dialog box, two headers and two footers (a total of four) may be defined in one document.

- Headers and Footers may be chosen from the Layout menu or the Format dialog box. They can be set to appear on every page, on odd pages, or on even pages.

- Headers and footers are created on a special Header/Footer screen. When you finish, F7 returns you to the working screen. Header and footer text does not appear on the working screen unless you are working in the Page mode, even though the codes can be seen in Reveal Codes.

- WordPerfect features such as bold, italics, underline, margins, center, and flush right may be used in headers and footers.

- Headers and footers may exceed one line. Headers begin at the top margin. Footers end at the bottom margin. The default setting separates a header or a footer from the text on the page by one blank line. WordPerfect automatically adjusts the number of lines of text on a page to make room for headers and footers.

- Headers and footers are considered page format codes. The Auto Code Placement feature will place a Header or Footer code at the top of the page on which the cursor is located when the header is created.

- Headers and footers are spell-checked along with your document.

- To edit a header or footer, change to the Page mode. Move through the document until you see the header or footer to be edited. Point to it and double-click. This takes you to the edit screen where you can make the correction and press F7 to exit. (You can also choose Edit from the Header or Footer dialog box.)

▶ PAGE NUMBERING

WordPerfect will automatically number the pages of your document. The command for page numbering can be part of the header, as in Exercise 1, or it can be inserted as a separate command.

Page Numbering is chosen from the Page Format dialog box. Go to the Page Format dialog box, choose **1** Page **N**umbering, and then **1** Page Number **P**osition. Look at the options available for the placement of the page number!

As with headers and footers, the page numbering code will be placed at the top of the page on which the cursor is located when the command is given. If you don't want the first page of a document numbered, you may give the Page Numbering command on the second page and set **2** Page **N**umber in the Page Numbering dialog box at **1**.

▶ SUPPRESS

If you want the first page counted but don't want the number or the header or footer to appear, you can insert a Suppress code on that page. The Suppress feature can be found near the bottom of the Page Format dialog box. WordPerfect allows you to choose from suppressing individual headers or footers or suppressing only the page numbering. (Page numbers that are part of a header, however, can only be suppressed when you suppress the entire header.)

As with headers and footers, page numbering and suppress are page formatting codes. WordPerfect will position them at the top of the page. We'll practice using both of these formatting tools in the review exercise at the end of the lesson.

▶ FOOTNOTES AND ENDNOTES

WordPerfect will automatically position and format your footnotes in your work. All you have to do is tell WordPerfect where you'd like the footnote reference number and key the text in the footnote.

Endnotes are similar to footnotes with regard to their creation. However, endnotes are not printed at the bottom of the appropriate page as are footnotes. Instead, endnotes are usually printed on a separate page at the end of a document.

Footnotes and endnotes can be chosen from the **L**ayout menu or from a special dialog box that opens when you press Ctrl-F7. When you select either Footnote or Endnote and choose to Create, you will see a blank screen, much like when you were creating the header in Exercise 1. The footnote or endnote numbers are automatically inserted by WordPerfect, both in your document and in the actual footnote or endnote. Let's practice these neat features.

▶ **EXERCISE 12-2**

1. Key the text in Figure 12-1 as the text for page 1 of a document. When you come to the location for the footnote, give the command to create a footnote (**Ctrl-F7**). The footnote should say: **This is the text for Footnote #1.**

| FIGURE 12-1

```
This is page 1 of a document that requires a footnote.[1]
This is the text that follows the footnote reference number
on page 1.
```

2. Press **Ctrl-Enter** to begin a new page.

3. Follow the instructions in Step 1, but change it to refer to "page 2" rather than "page 1." Include another footnote for the second page.

Now let's give this two-page document a header and a page number. The header will be suppressed on the first page.

> **EXERCISE 12-3**

1. Go to the Header/Footer/Watermark dialog box and tell WordPerfect that you'd like to put Header A on every page of your document. For the header, key **Practice Document** at the left. Return to your working screen.

2. Go to the Page Format dialog box and choose Page **N**umbering. Put a page number at bottom center of every page.

3. Return to your working screen and look at both pages of the document in Print Pre**v**iew. Press **Page Down** to move to the second page. Is the header in place on each page? Are the page numbers centered at the bottom of the pages? How do the footnotes look?

4. Close Print Pre**v**iew and change to the Page mode. Look at the header, footer, and footnotes. (Footnote 2 and the page number at the bottom of the second page are not displayed because the text on the page is short. The only way you can see them using the Page mode is to press **Home, Home** ↓ to go to the bottom of your document and add another hard page break using **Ctrl-Enter** to start Page 3.)

5. Position your cursor on the first page of the document. Return to the Page Format dialog box and choose **9 Su**ppress. Select *Header A*. Press **Home, F7** to return directly to your document. Now check for all of the extra parts in your document. Was the header suppressed on the first page only?

6. Print your two-page document. Then close it, saving it as **foot**.

As you can see, footnotes are as easy to add as headers and page numbers, and WordPerfect takes care of the numbering and the formatting. Here is some additional miscellaneous information about footnotes.

- Footnotes or endnotes are most easily entered as you key the document—key to the point of the note, give the proper command and enter the text of the note, and then use F7 to return to the document to continue keying.

- If you wish to delete a footnote or endnote, move the cursor to the reference number in the text and delete it. WordPerfect will delete the note and automatically renumber the remaining notes.

- If you move text that affects footnotes or endnotes, WordPerfect will automatically renumber the notes.

- If you use endnotes, you must put an Endnote Placement code wherever you'd like the endnotes to be placed. As with footnotes, endnotes won't show on the screen unless you are in the Page mode or in Print Pre**v**iew.

- To edit a footnote or endnote, change to the Page mode. Move through the document until you see the "note" to be edited. Point to the note and double-click. This takes you to the edit screen where you can make the correction and press F7 to exit. (You can also choose Edit from the Footnote or Endnote dialog box.)

PAGE END CONTROL

Occasionally you will create a document that has some awkward page endings. For example, a single line of a paragraph at the bottom or the top of a page is usually not desirable. These single lines are called widows and orphans. At other times, a side heading might fall at the end of a page with the accompanying text on the next page. On still other occasions, you might want to keep entire name and address segments together on one page.

WordPerfect provides you with three tools to help control those page endings—Widow/Orphan Protect, Block Protect, and Conditional End of Page. All three of these choices can be made from the Other Format dialog box. Open that dialog box and look at it now.

Widow/Orphan Protect takes care of the single lines of a paragraph at the bottom or top of a page. If the problem is a single line at the bottom of a page, that line is moved to the next page. If the problem is a single line at the top of a page, the preceding line of the paragraph will be moved to the following page to accompany the single line.

When creating a multiple-page document, you may make it part of your regular routine (along with headers, footers, page numbering and/or suppress) to choose Widow/Orphan Protect from the Other Format dialog box. Then, regardless of the editing you do in the document, you can be certain you won't have any widow or orphans in your documents.

Block Protect is more often used when you are working with a random section of text that must be kept together on one page. You can usually see when a page break is going to come in an awkward spot, for example in a table or an address. When that happens, simply block the text that should be kept together and choose Block Protect from the Other Format dialog box. WordPerfect will move the entire block to the next page. Block Protect can also be used to bind side headings to one or two lines of the text that follows and keep them together on one page.

Conditional End of Page works much like Block Protect except that with Conditional End of Page, you must tell WordPerfect how many lines to keep together.

▶ OTHER FEATURES

WordPerfect provides a number of other features useful for multiple-page documents. The Mark Text feature enables you to mark the text to be included in a Table of Contents or a list. With the text marked, you can automatically generate the appropriate list.

The Master Document feature provides a "shell" with which you can tie a number of documents together. Then you can print or generate lists without actually combining the documents into one large file.

▶ SUMMARY

You learned some of the most important features to be used in multiple-page documents–headers, footers, page numbering, footnotes, and endnotes. While you have not yet practiced all of the features mentioned in this lesson, you will find all of them easy to use. A longer exercise at the end of this lesson provides more realistic practice than the little exercises in the lesson. Also, the *WordPerfect Reference* contains additional information about all of these features, and the *WordPerfect Workbook* includes some exercises.

LESSON 12 NOTES:

LESSON 11 & 12 ACTIVITIES

LESSON 11

1. Where in your letter must you position the cursor when you wish to use the Envelope feature to prepare an envelope?

2. If you wish to include the POSTNET bar code on envelopes or labels prepared in a merge, how must you set up the data file?

3. Which would give you the larger labels, 3" x 10" labels or 2" x 7" labels?

4. Where must the Paper Size/Type code be placed in the form file to prepare laser labels?

5. What are the three kinds of WordPerfect Sort listed in the Record Type pop-up box? (Just for your information, if you are in a table when you give the Sort command, WordPerfect will open a Table Sort dialog box that looks just like the regular one.)

6. What is the difference between an *Alpha* Sort and a *Num* Sort?

7. How do you fool WordPerfect into thinking two names are only one name for the purposes of a sort?

8. When using Select, you must key the Select criteria. Then WordPerfect has to find the field to be considered for the Select. How do you direct WordPerfect to the right field?

ACTIVITY

LESSON 12

1. What is the difference between a header and a footer? How many total headers and footers can you have in a single document? Are you apt to use that many?

2. If you want the pages of your document numbered but don't want to include the page number in the header, what WordPerfect feature can you use to number the pages?

3. You can tell WordPerfect to number the pages of your document using the Page Numbering command. Within what other feature can you put a Page Numbering code? What is the keystroke that tells WordPerfect to put a page number at a specific location?

4. What feature is used to keep page numbers, headers, or footers from appearing on a particular page?

5. What is the difference between a footnote and an endnote? Can you have both in one document?

6. Name the three features that can be used to prevent page breaks in undesirable locations?

Reference Questions. Near the end of the Page Numbering section of the *WordPerfect Reference* is a discussion of Complex Page Numbering Schemes. How many pieces of identification are included in the sample "page number."

Turn to the Footnotes section of the *Reference*. What will happen if you put a footnote in a column?

The *Reference* tells you that you can put footnotes in a table but not in a table header row. Look in the Index of the *Reference* to find the section on Tables, Header Rows. What is a table header row?

124 **ACTIVITY**

REVIEW

Open **deskpub** from the template disk, OR:

Key the manuscript in Figure 12-2.

1. If you key the manuscript, add the footnotes as you go. If you open the manuscript from the template files, move the cursor to the proper location and add the footnotes to the text. The footnotes are illustrated at the end of the manuscript.

Format the document as follows:

2. The document should be double-spaced, with a quadruple space following the title.

3. The title should be keyed in all capital letters 2 inches from the top of the paper. (Don't change the top margin setting. Instead, use **Enter** to move the cursor to **Pos 2"** for the title.)

4. Give the document a header, **Desktop Publishing**. Automatically number the pages of the document, with the numeral appearing in the upper right corner. (You may use the Page Numbering feature or include the page number as part of your header.)

5. Neither the page number nor the header should appear on the first page. (Use Suppress.)

6. Set Widow/Orphan Protect to aid in proper pagination.

7. Use Print Preview to make sure everything is correct in your document before printing.

8. Print the document and close it, saving it as **deskpub.for** so you can differentiate between the formatted document and the one that contains no formatting.

FIGURE 12-2

DESKTOP PUBLISHING

It is nearly impossible today to look at a trade publication or a seminar flyer and not see something about desktop publishing. Articles and seminars abound. Corporate personnel, administrators, and business educators are inundated with information on how desktop publishing can be a big help for their companies. Millions of advertising dollars are being poured into promotion of desktop publishing, and new software is being released regularly to enable users to create their own fancy documents using desktop publishing software.[1]

Desktop publishing is the term used to describe an arrangement where a personal computer-based system or a dedicated work station uses page layout software to output documents to a laser printer.[2] Usually the page layout software includes text processing capabilities coupled with extensive graphics capabilities allowing the user to combine text formatted into any kind of column layout with graphics, to see it on the screen, and to ultimately send it to the printer with WYSIWYG (what you see is what you get) accuracy.

The laser printer enhances the process because of its ability to produce fine graphic images on the same page as the text.[3]

This whole area of desktop publishing is important because companies, large and small, pay large amounts of money to have professional looking pages of copy produced for in-house manuals, advertising brochures, instructional booklets, etc. It is estimated that an average of $72 million is paid annually by EACH of the Fortune 500 companies for this process.[4] In addition to the actual outlay of cash that can be saved, time savings, control, and security are all important considerations to companies contemplating doing their document production within the confines of their organizations!

(Here are the footnotes for you to key at the proper locations in the text.)

[1] "Desktop Publishing Strikes a New Chord," *Floor Avenue Report*, May 18, 1993, p. 17.

[2] Peter Addison, "Laser Graphics Hit the Spot," *Technology Review*, June 1992, p. 37.

[3] "Big Business Benefits from Desktop Publishing," *Corporate Review*, July 1991, p. 47.

[4] *Ibid.*, p. 19.

LESSON 13

Using Macros

OBJECTIVES

Upon completion of this lesson, you will be able to:

1. Create and use macros.
2. Discuss general macro information.
3. Edit a macro.

Estimated Time: 1/2 hour

A macro is one way of saving a series of keystrokes that you use with regularity. By using macros, you can speed up your work. Macros are used to store frequently used phrases, paragraphs, and complicated formats. Creating a macro involves the following three steps:

1. Naming the macro,
2. Keying the information or format steps to be saved, and
3. Ending the macro.

   When you end the macro, it is saved on your disk. At that point, you may use it as often as you wish.

CREATING AND PLAYING A MACRO

In the first exercise you'll learn to create a simple macro you could use for your business correspondence—providing you worked for the Werneck Gesthaus Posthotel.

EXERCISE 13-1

1. Press **Ctrl-F10**. The Record Macro dialog box will appear, asking for the name of the macro. Key **wg** and press **Enter**. *Recording Macro* will appear in the lower left corner of the screen.

2. Turn on Bold. Then key **Werneck Gesthaus Posthotel**. Do not put a period or a space at the end. Turn off Bold.

3. End the macro by pressing **Ctrl-F10** again. Close the document without saving.

4. Key the paragraph illustrated in Figure 13-1. Each time you come to the name of the hotel, press **Alt-F10** and key **wg**. Then press **Enter**. The words in your macro should automatically appear in bold on the screen!

5. Proofread. Then print your document and close it, saving it as **gesthaus**.

FIGURE 13-1

> Thank you for choosing the **Werneck Gesthaus Posthotel** for your home away from home as you travel through Germany. The staff and management of the **Werneck Gesthaus Posthotel** would like to see to all of your needs. Please allow us to serve you.
>
> The dining room of the **Werneck Gesthaus Posthotel** is open from 7:15 a.m. until 10 p.m. for your dining pleasure. Bring your family and friends and experience the excellence of food served in true Bavarian tradition.
>
> After you move on in your travels, we would like you to remember the good times you had while you were a guest at the **Werneck Gesthaus Posthotel** so that you will stay with us when you return to the area.

Wasn't that fun? You now have enough knowledge to create and use macros in all of your work. It's simply a matter of capturing the keystrokes and then reusing them as many times as needed.

MACRO INFORMATION

Here are some miscellaneous pieces of macro information:

- There are two kinds of macros—named macros and Alt macros.
  - A **named** macro is named using eight or fewer characters. You just worked with a named macro. It is created using Ctrl-F10, keying the name, and then collecting the keystrokes. It is run by pressing Alt-F10 and keying the macro name.

128 LESSON 13 USING MACROS

- An **Alt** macro is created in the same way as a named macro except the name of an Alt macro includes an Alt-character keystroke. When naming Alt macros, be careful to avoid using the alphabetic letters that open one of the WordPerfect 6.0 menus. We'll try an Alt macro shortly.

- Macros are automatically stored with a **.wpm** extension. The default location for macros is the **C:\WP60\MACROS** directory. Yours may be set to save on your disk so they are available on whatever machine you choose to use.

- Macros can be edited like a regular document. We'll also try that shortly.

- You can delete a macro from in the File Manager, just like you'd delete an ordinary document.

▶ **EXERCISE 13-2**

1. Press **Ctrl-F10** to create a macro. At the *Macro Name* prompt, press **Alt-r** for **r**eturn address or lette**r** and press **Enter**. Check the lower left corner of the screen for the words *Recording Macro*.

2. Press **Enter** six times to give your letter a 2-inch top margin.

3. Key your street address and press **Enter**. Key your city, state, and ZIP code and press **Enter** again.

4. Press **Shift-F5** and choose **2** Date **C**ode so the current date will automatically be inserted at the top of each of your letters (providing the clock in your computer is correctly set).

   *Choose **D**ate and then **C**ode from the **T**ools menu.*

5. Press **Enter** four more times to leave the minimum of three blank lines between the date and the inside address.

6. Press **Ctrl-F10** again to end the recording of your macro. Then clear your screen without saving.

7. Press **Alt-r** to run your macro. Did it work? If not, repeat the exercise. If so, you can clear the screen and move on.

The top margin on the macro you just created is too deep and you'd like two additional blank lines between the date and the inside address. You could re-create the macro. Instead, let's edit it. In WordPerfect 6.0, macros can be opened and edited like regular documents (providing you know how to key the commands in exactly the correct way), or you can give the command to create the macro, use the same name, and choose to edit.

▶ **EXERCISE 13-3a**

1. Press **Ctrl-F10** and press **Alt-r**. A dialog box will tell you that a macro already exists with that name. Choose to Edit it. The document that appears should look much like Figure 13-2 except that the generic information will be replaced with your return address.

LESSON 13 USING MACROS **129**

FIGURE 13-2
Macro Text

```
DISPLAY(Off!)
HardReturn
HardReturn
HardReturn
HardReturn
HardReturn
HardReturn
Type{"(your address)"}
HardReturn
Type{"(your city, state, ZIP code)"}
HardReturn
DateCode
HardReturn
HardReturn
HardReturn
HardReturn
```

2. Move the cursor to the *HardReturn* lines above your street address and delete two of them. Delete the blank lines, too.

3. Press **Page Down** to move the cursor to the bottom of the macro to add two more hard returns. You may add hard returns in one of two ways:

   - If you opened the macro like a regular document, you may key the words **HardReturn**, putting each on a separate line.

   - If you entered the macro through the Edit Macro process, you may follow the prompt at the bottom of the screen to press **Shift-F3** to move to a blank screen where you can enter the keystrokes to be included in the macro. In this case, you would press **Shift-F3**, press **Enter** twice, and press **Shift-F3** to return to the Edit Macro screen. The two additional hard returns would show in your macro.

4. Choose your method and add two more hard returns to the bottom of your macro.

5. Save the macro again with the same name in the normal manner and close it. Clear the screen and run the macro again. Check the spacing to see if everything is OK.

Now let's assume you'd like this to be a modified block style letter, with the return address and date lines beginning at approximately center. You need to add six Tab codes before each of the lines of the return address and date.

▶ **EXERCISE 13-3b**

1. Open your **Alt-r** macro again and position the cursor at the beginning of the *street address* line. Press **Ctrl-F3** and press **Tab** six times. Press **Ctrl-F3** to return to the Edit Macro screen. Look at the results.

2. Follow the same procedure to add the tabs to the city, state, and ZIP code line. Don't worry about the tabs that are already on that screen. Then follow the procedure to add tabs before the date.

3. Follow the usual procedure to save the document with the same name. Then press **Alt-r** to run the macro again. Do your introductory lines begin at approximately center (**Pos 4"**)? If not, your macro may need further editing.

4. Close the document without saving.

▶ CHAINED AND NESTED MACROS

Quite a number of merge and macro codes are available that enable you to do some pretty fantastic things with macros. For example, you can nest one macro somewhere in the middle of another macro, or you can chain macros by putting the command to start *macro b* at the end of *macro a*. If you have some ingenuity, you can set up some pretty sophisticated applications.

The WordPerfect macro manual is a separate document that ships on disk with WordPerfect. To access macro help, choose **M**acros from the **H**elp menu. You can read the information on the screen or it can be printed for reference purposes.

▶ MACRO LISTS

You will save yourself much time and frustration by keeping track of your macros. Make a list. You can start with a list of the letters of the alphabet for your Alt macros. Cross off those letters that are used for pull-down menus. Then write in a description of each macro assigned to an alphabetic character as you create it. Keep a list of macros that are named, including a short description of each. Put your macro list in a place where it will be readily available for reference or to add new macros.

▶ SUMMARY

In this lesson you learned two methods of creating macros. You also learned to edit them. Macros are a major source of saved time only IF you remember to use them. If you are alert to situations calling for repetitive keystrokes, you will remember to create macros for those situations and save yourself much time and trouble.

LESSON 13 NOTES:

LESSON 14

WordPerfect Columns and Outlines

OBJECTIVES

Upon completion of this lesson, you will be able to:

1. Format your text using Newspaper Columns.
2. Discuss Parallel Columns.
3. Use the Automatic Outline feature.

Estimated Time: 3/4 hour

You learned in Lesson 9 that the WordPerfect Table feature is an excellent way to create certain kinds of columnar work. A better way to create some kinds of text columns, however, is with the WordPerfect Columns feature. When you choose Columns from the **L**ayout menu or choose it by pressing Alt-F7 and **1 C**olumns, you are presented with four different kinds of columns and a variety of setup options. Go to the Text Columns dialog box and look at the choices.

The Newspaper and Balanced Newspaper columns choice would be used for the kinds of columns you see in magazines and newspapers. We'll explore those choices first.

▶ NEWSPAPER COLUMNS

Newspaper columns "snake" from one column to the next. When the first column is filled, the text spills over to the next column. When all of the columns on a page are filled, the text spills over into the first column of the next page.

When you don't have enough text to fill a page and would like the columns to end evenly, Balanced Newspaper Columns will do the job for you very nicely. Let's practice.

▶ **EXERCISE 14-1**

1. Open **columns** from the template disk, OR:

Key the text in Figure 14-1. This is a relatively short document.

| **FIGURE 14-1**

```
One of the features that has made WordPerfect such a popular
text editor is the flexible columns feature.  When you use
WordPerfect columns, you may create as many as 24 side-by-
side columns.

One kind of WordPerfect column is Newspaper Columns, where
the text snakes (wraps) from the bottom of one column to the
top of the next.  Closely related to newspaper columns is
the feature called Balanced Newspaper Columns.  With
balanced columns, a short page of text ends evenly at the
bottom of both columns.

With parallel columns, related sections of text can be
printed side by side across the page.  In Parallel Columns
with Block Protect, the Block Protect prevents awkward page
breaks.

With both Newspaper and Parallel columns, WordPerfect
assumes equal column sizes and figures the column margins
with whatever text margins are set.  The default settings
allow a half-inch space called a "gutter" between columns.
Text can be added to or deleted from the columns, and the
integrity of the columns is not destroyed.
```

2. Use **Page Up** to move the cursor to the top of the text. Press **Alt-F7**, choose **1 C**olumns, and then press **Enter** to choose the default, which is Newspaper. Look at your text. It fills about two-thirds of the first column on the page. You may wish to look at it in Print Pre**v**iew.

3. Now let's change to Balanced Newspaper Columns. Press **Alt-F7**, choose **1 C**olumns, **1 T**ype, and **2** Balanced N**e**wspaper. Return to your document and look at it. It should look much like the portion of a document illustrated in Figure 14-2.

> One of the features that has made WordPerfect such a popular text editor is the flexible columns feature. When you use WordPerfect columns, you may create as many as 24 side-by-side columns.
>
> One kind of WordPerfect column is Newspaper Columns, where the text snakes (wraps) from the bottom of one column to the top of the next. Closely related to newspaper columns is the feature called Balanced Newspaper Columns. With balanced columns, a short page of text ends evenly at the bottom of both columns.
>
> With Parallel Columns, related sections of text can be printed side by side across the page. In Parallel Columns with Block Protect, the Block Protect prevents awkward page breaks.
>
> With both Newspaper and Parallel columns, WordPerfect assumes equal column sizes and figures the column margins with whatever text margins are set. The default settings allow a half-inch space called a "gutter" between columns. Text can be added to or deleted from the columns, and the integrity of the columns is not destroyed.

4. Print your document and save it as **columns.1**. Keep it open on the screen.

That was a quick introduction to Columns. Now let's change where the columns begin. We'll do this by moving the code. (You can move codes just like you move text in your documents!)

▶ EXERCISE 14-2

1. Reveal your codes and press **Page Up** to position the cursor directly after the [Col Def] code. Press **Backspace** to remove the code.

2. Move your cursor to the beginning of the second paragraph. Press **Esc** or choose **U**ndelete from the **E**dit menu and then **1 R**estore to put the code into the document at the position of the cursor.

3. Practice moving the cursor from column to column. If you use the mouse, you can simply point and click the cursor into position. If you don't use a mouse, you can move from the column at the left to the column at the right with **Ctrl-Home** and then →.

4. Print this version of your columns document and close it, saving it as **columns.2**.

The Newspaper Columns feature gives you lots of flexibility. For example, if you are using regular Newspaper Columns, you can set different size columns by choosing the Custom Widths button in the Text Columns dialog box and editing the column sizes as well as the space between columns there.

PARALLEL COLUMNS

An entirely different kind of column that is defined in the same menu as the newspaper-style columns is Parallel Columns. This feature keeps groups of information together horizontally. Parallel Columns might be used for scripts, itineraries, or listings of inventory.

Figure 14-3 illustrates an example of material in Parallel Columns. Following the figure is some information about Parallel Columns.

FIGURE 14-3

```
Employee         This document was prepared to    Mary Jones
Protection       tell about the new employee
Plan             protection plan devised for
                 all employees.  It was created
                 on January 14, 1966.

Employee         This document tells about the    Maria
Assistance       Employee Assistance Plan to      Rafferty
Plan             help employees in trouble.  It
                 was created on June 11, 1986.
```

- Each segment is keyed continuously. The text wraps within the column until you press Ctrl-Enter for a hard page break. At that point, the cursor moves to the next column.

- You may have as many as 24 columns across the page.

- You can go to the Define menu to set columns at any size, as long as they fit on the page. They may be of equal or unequal widths.

- The Block Protect feature keeps horizontal items together. For example, if the Employee Assistance Plan information in Figure 14-3 didn't all fit on one page, Block Protect would cause the entire segment to be moved to the next page.

- Many of the things you might use Parallel Columns for could be done more easily using the Tables feature. THINK before using a WordPerfect feature!

OUTLINING

The WordPerfect Outlining feature contains a number of preset outline styles. These include the normal outline with Roman numerals, a paragraph numbering style, and a bullet style as well as some legal styles. The paragraph numbering style is the default, and you can start an outline of that type simply by pressing Ctrl-t.

1. Press **Ctrl-t** to start an outline. The first numeral should appear, followed by an →Indent code so the text wraps to the right place.

2. Key the little sample in Figure 14-4. After keying **WordPerfect 6.0,** press **Enter** twice. The next numeral will appear the first time you press **Enter**. The second time is to insert a blank line.

3. Press **Tab** to indent to the next level of the outline and key the text for *a*. Then press **Enter** and key the text for *b*.

4. Press **Enter** twice and then **Shift-Tab** to change the *c.* back to a *2*. Key the last line of the outline and press **Enter**. Then press **Ctrl-t** to turn off the outline.

5. Print the outline. Close it, saving it as **outline.1** and read on to learn more about outlining.

▶ **EXERCISE 14-3**

```
1.  This is a sample of the first level of an outline using
    WordPerfect 6.0.
    a.  This is a sample of the second level of the little
        outline.
    b.  This is the second level, too.
2.  This is the end of the outline.
```

FIGURE 14-4

If you want to work with one of the other styles of outlining or wish to change the defaults, press Ctrl-F5 to open the Outline dialog box. It should look like Figure 14-5.

Choose **O**utline and then Out**l**ine Options from the **T**ools menu.

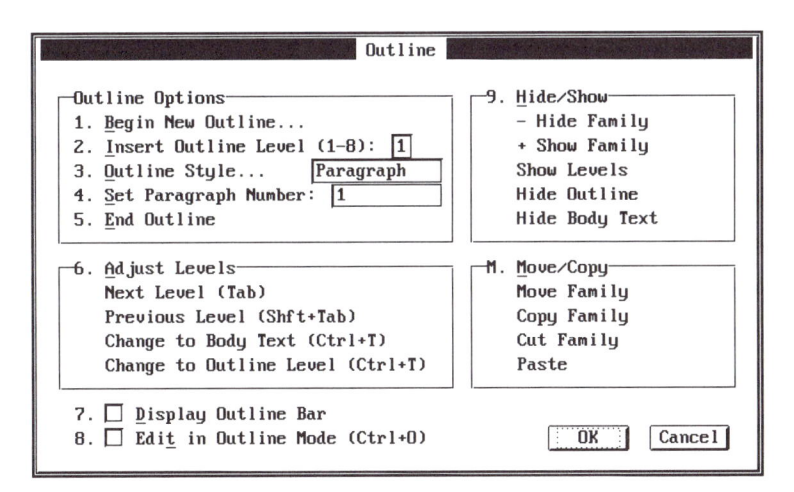

FIGURE 14-5
Outline Dialog Box

Look at the dialog box. In Section 6, you'll see the four features you've already used. Section M deals with moving and copying sections of the outline. When you move, copy, cut, or paste a portion of an outline, the items will renumber automatically.

Section 9 of the dialog box deals with a feature that enables the user to temporarily collapse the outline, showing only those levels desired. For example, display and print only the numbered sections of the outline in Figure 14-4 and hide the lettered sections. If you work much with outlines, you will want to "play" with this feature.

LESSON 14 WORDPERFECT COLUMNS AND OUTLINES **137**

In the Outline Options section, you can choose the style of outline you wish to create and a number of other options. Keep the dialog box open and we'll try another exercise.

> **EXERCISE 14-4**

1. Choose either **1 B**egin New Outline or **3 O**utline Style to bring up the list of preset outline styles.

2. Choose Bullets and return to your document screen. Key the little outline in Figure 14-4 again. The procedure is the same. You will see two levels of bullets in your exercise.

3. Print the bullet outline and close it, saving it as **outline.2**.

4. Now return to the Outline dialog box and choose the Outline Style. Key the exercise in Figure 14-4 one more time. When you get to the end, add the additional text in Figure 14-6. Press **Enter** once at the end of the final item and then press **Ctrl-t** to end the outline.

5. Print this outline and save it as **outline.3**. Keep it open on the screen.

> **FIGURE 14-6**

```
III. This is another item at the first level.  The Roman
     numerals are beginning to get a little crowded.  I can
     fix the Roman numerals in one of two ways.

     A.  I can reset the distance between the left margin
         and the first tab stop so there is room for my
         Roman numerals.
         1.   Delete the tab stop at 0.5".
         2.   Set a tab stop at 0.8".
     B.  I can create an outline style that uses a decimal
         tab for the first level of the outline.  In that
         way the Roman numerals will be aligned at the
         decimal.

IV.  I think I am finally finished with this outline.  Even
     though most outlines aren't made up of complete
     sentences, this outline looks great!
```

EDITING OUTLINES

As mentioned before, not only can outlines be created easily, they can be edited with great ease, too. You can move sections around, add sections, and delete sections. Let's learn as we practice.

> **EXERCISE 14-5**

1. Position the cursor somewhere in the final item of the outline and press **Ctrl-o** to open the Outline Editor. The entire final item will be highlighted, and the outline bar will appear at the top of the screen. The outline bar provides quite a number of editing options.

2. Hold **Ctrl** while you press → once. See how easy it is to change the level of an item. Now reverse the process—press **Ctrl** ← to change it back to a Roman numeral item.

3. Hold **Ctrl** while you press ↑ twice. Now it is the second item in the outline, and everything that needs to be renumbered has automatically been changed.

4. Follow the necessary steps to make the following changes to your outline.

    a. Make the current second item (the one you just moved) the next-to-last item in the outline.

    b. Make the original second item (the one-liner) the very last item in the outline.

    c. Change around the A and B sections of II so the "style" section is A and the "reset distance" section is B.

5. With the "finally finished" section highlighted, press **Delete** to remove that section. Press **Ctrl-o** to exit the Outline Editor.

6. Position the cursor at the end of the B section of the first item. Press **Enter** twice. Then press **Shift-Tab**. A new Roman numeral II will appear and those following it will be renumbered. Key something about this being the second item at the first level.

7. Make sure the spacing surrounding all of the items is correct. If you need to press **Enter** to add a blank line, a new numeral will be added. You may simply backspace to remove the numeral code.

8. Look at the codes in your document. Note that there are really no numerals—just codes. When your outline is lovely, print it and save it as **outline.4**. Keep it open on the screen.

Finally, let's learn about collapsing an outline.

> **EXERCISE 14-6**

1. Press **Ctrl-o** to enter the Outline Editor again.

2. Choose the **S**how button on the Outline bar. Then key **1** to display ONLY Level 1. Notice the + and – symbols in front of the items. Can you guess what those symbols are telling you?

3. Choose **S**how and **2**. What is still missing from the outline?

4. Finally, choose **S**how and **A**ll. Close the document without saving.

There are other options on the Outline Bar that you can read about in the *WordPerfect Reference* or try on your own. You should be very good with outlines at this point.

SUMMARY

Text Columns and Outlines—these are a couple of WordPerfect features that should make your life more exciting because they are so easy to use. In the next lesson you're going to use the Columns feature again as you learn to use the Graphics features of WordPerfect.

LESSON 14 NOTES:

ACTIVITY

LESSON 13 & 14 ACTIVITIES

LESSON 13

1. What appears in the lower left corner of the screen when you are keying the keystrokes to be included in a macro?

2. What keystrokes must you use to play a named macro?

3. When naming an Alt macro, what alphabetic letters must you avoid? Why?

4. What keystrokes do you press if you wish to play a macro named **Alt-x**?

5. When you want to edit a macro, what keystrokes take you to a blank WordPerfect screen where you can key the strokes to be added to the macro? What keystrokes take you back to your macro edit screen?

6. What is the extension that WordPerfect applies to all macros?

7. Think of something you do on a regular basis that could be done more easily with a macro. Describe the example and give the steps to create a macro to enhance your work.

ACTIVITY

LESSON 14

1. What is the difference between Newspaper Columns and Balanced Newspaper Columns?

2. What is the maximum number of side-by-side columns allowed by WordPerfect?

3. Would 24 columns fit better on paper that was turned in the portrait orientation or in the landscape orientation?

4. What is the word used to describe the space between columns? How large is that space if you use the default settings?

5. What is the default outline style in WordPerfect 6.0 for DOS? If you want to use that style, what keystrokes will start (and end) an outline?

6. How do you go from a first-level indent to a second-level indent? How do you return from a second-level indent to a first-level indent?

7. Where must you go to be able to automatically edit an outline? What keystrokes take you to that point? What appears at the top of the screen when you are there?

Reference Questions. Turn to the Macro section of the *WordPerfect Reference*. On the third page, what does the *Reference* say must be done before WordPerfect can play a macro

Turn in the Outline section of the *Reference* to the discussion about Hiding/Showing All Body Text. Read that section. Then turn to the next-to-last page of the section and look at the illustration of a document that contains body text. What outline style is used in that illustration? How many levels were used—in addition to the body text?

142 ACTIVITY

LESSON 15

WordPerfect Graphics

OBJECTIVES

Upon completion of this lesson, you will be able to:

1. Insert and format a graphics image.
2. Use graphics lines to enhance your documents.
3. Use borders in your documents.
4. Use the Equation Editor.

Estimated Time: 1/2 hour

When formatting documents for business or personal use, the "designer" of the document often uses what graphics tools are available to enhance the appearance of the document. WordPerfect has helped you in document layout by making it easy to insert and position graphics images, borders, and graphics lines in your documents.

GRAPHICS BOXES

WordPerfect 6.0 for DOS is shipped with 34 graphics images. The program also contains eight predetermined styles for those images. The styles that ship with the program can be modified or you can create your own style, if you wish.

Two of the styles deal with equations. We'll work with equations later in the lesson. One of the styles is a watermark. You can play with watermarks and Button Boxes on your own. The other four styles have definite characteristics. Let's learn about them. Figure Boxes, Table Boxes, Text Boxes, and User Boxes may contain text or an image retrieved from one of the versions of WordPerfect, from clip art, or scanned from hard copy. The boxes can be sized and positioned wherever you'd like them on the page.

FIGURE BOX

A figure box has a single line on all four sides and a caption, if you'd like, at the bottom of the box. Figure 15-1 illustrates a graphics image in a figure box.

FIGURE 15-1
Figure Box

TABLE BOX

The main characteristic that sets table boxes apart from the other box styles is that the figure or text is contained in two heavy black lines–one at the top and one at the bottom. The caption for a table box is at the top of the box. Figure 15-2 illustrates a table box with tabular material.

FIGURE 15-2
Table Box

TEXT BOX

Text boxes are just like table boxes except that the background is shaded and the caption is at the bottom. You can set the percentage of shading to achieve just the right look. Figure 15-3 illustrates a text box.

FIGURE 15-3
Text Box

USER BOX

User boxes don't have any lines around them. When no caption is used, a figure in a user box appears to be free floating in the document. If you use a caption, the default location is below the box at the left. Figure 15-4 illustrates a user box containing a graphics image.

FIGURE 15-4
User Box

BUTTON BOX

A button box looks just like one of the buttons in the dialog boxes with which you have been working. You can put buttons into your documents and link them to hypertext. Then you can create company manuals in WordPerfect with buttons in the table of contents that, when clicked, will take the user directly to the section referenced. Amazing! Figure 15-5 illustrates a button box.

FIGURE 15-5
Button Box

CREATE A GRAPHICS BOX

You are probably anxious to try your hand with graphics. Let's create a figure box and put a graphics image in the box. For this first exercise, we will use all of the default settings.

1. Press **Alt-F9** for the Graphics dialog box. Choose **1** Graphics **B**oxes and **1 C**reate. A dialog box will appear that looks like Figure 15-6. Look at Section **Y** at the bottom. Note that Figure Box is the default.

▶ **EXERCISE 15-1**

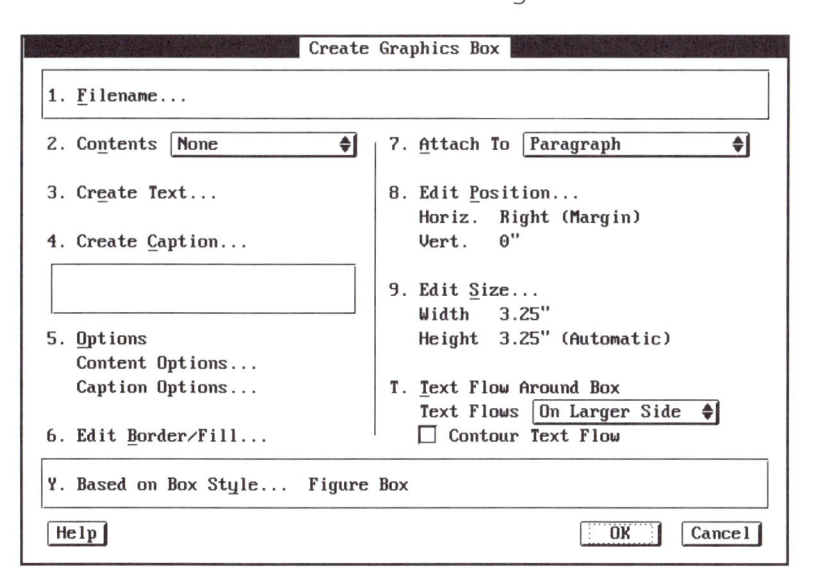

Open the **G**raphics menu. Choose Graphics **B**oxes and **C**reate.

FIGURE 15-6
Create Graphics Box Dialog Box

2. Choose **1 F**ilename. Key **c:\wp60\graphics\fishtrop.wpg** and press **Enter**. This tells the computer to look in the Graphics subdirectory of the WP60 directory on Drive C which is where your graphics images normally are installed. If a *File Not Found* alert box appears, ask your instructor for help in locating the graphics images.

3. When **fishtrop.wpg** appears on the Filename line, choose OK to return to your document.

4. Your graphic will fill the upper right quarter of the page. If you are working on a color monitor, your fish should appear in color. (If you have a color printer, you can even print your fish in color!)

5. Print the document and save it as **fish.1**. Keep the document open.

Now that you've learned to put a graphic into your document, let's see what else you can do with that graphic.

▶ EXERCISE 15-2

1. Press **Alt-F9** and choose **1** Graphics **B**oxes. Then choose **2 E**dit. A dialog box will ask you which graphic you would like to edit. The prompt is *Box 1*. Press **Enter**.

2. The Edit Graphics Box dialog box looks very much like the box in Figure 15-6. Choose **8** Edit **P**osition and set Horizontal Position at Left.

3. Choose **9** Edit **S**ize and set the Width at **1.5"**. Leave the Height setting at Automatic. (If you set both, you won't distort the image, but the box around it may be snug on all four sides.)

4. Choose **4** Create **C**aption and key **My Pet Fish**. Follow the prompt to press **F7** to return to the Edit dialog box.

5. Choose **5 O**ptions and then **2 C**aption Options. For **1 S**ide of Box, choose Left. For **3 P**osition, choose Center. For **7 R**otation, choose 90 degrees. Choose OK.

6. Choose **T**ext Flow and then Contour Text Flow. Then close the Edit Graphics dialog box.

7. Open your File Manager and find a small text document. **Gesthaus** should work fine. Use Retrieve to bring the document into the document you currently have open. Does the text wrap around the fish? It should.

8. Return to your document screen and look at your fish. Print a copy and save it as **fish.2**. Keep the document open. Notice that the box is missing from around the fish. That's because you chose Contour. Text would look pretty funny printing over the line around the box.

Move the mouse pointer anywhere on the fish and double-click to open the Edit Graphics Box dialog box.

You're doing great. Now let's see what can be done with an image in the Image Editor.

▶ EXERCISE 15-3

1. Return to the Edit Graphics Box dialog box and choose **3** Image **E**ditor.

2. Choose **B**rightness and set it at **0.5**. If you'd print, this fish would not be quite as dark. (In fact, you could make it really light and use it as a watermark behind your documents. More on watermarks later.)

3. Choose Scale **W**idth and set it at **2.0**. Then press → a few times until the lips of your fish show. (This is about the only way you can crop an image–move the unwanted part out of the image box.)

4. Play with some of the other options in the Image Editor. Then press **Ctrl-Home** or choose Reset All from the Button Bar at the top of the Editor to return the fish to its original position and size.

5. It is poor design to have an image looking off the page. Choose Flip **H**oriz to turn your fish around.

6. Press **F7** or click **Close** to return to the Edit dialog box. Then press **Home, F7** to return to your document. It should look much like the partial page in Figure 15-7. Print the document and save it as **fish.3**.

FIGURE 15-7
Document With Image

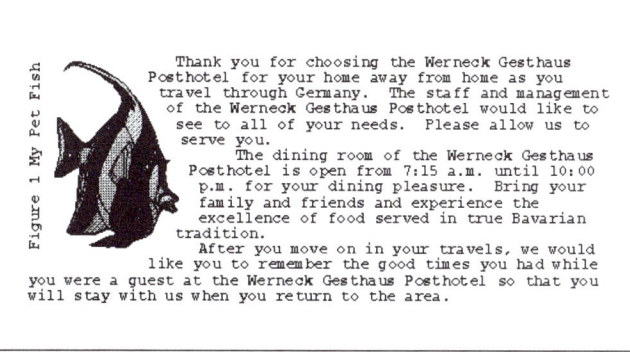

7. If you have a mouse, point to the fish and click once. The image should have a dotted line and eight "sizing handles." When the pointer is on the image, it is a four-headed arrow. Press the left mouse button and use that tool to drag the fish image around on the screen. Wherever you release the button, that's where the fish will stay.

8. Point to any one of the handles. The pointer should turn to a double-headed arrow. Drag that handle to change the size of the image. If you grab a corner handle, you can change both height and width at the same time. Play a little. Then close the document without saving.

ATTACH TO

Graphics boxes can be attached to the Page (they stay in the same place, regardless of what happens to the text around them). They can be attached to a Paragraph (as text is edited and the paragraph moves, the graphic moves with the text). When you attach a graphics image to a character, it stays with that character, wherever the character goes on the page. As you work with graphics, you'll find reasons to use all three of these options.

TEXT IN BOXES

When you would like text in a graphics box of any kind, choose **3 Cr**e**ate** Text in the Create Graphics Box dialog box. You'll be taken to a narrow box to key your text (or paste text you might have cut or copied from another document). You can adjust the size of the box after you've returned to your document. When you are putting the text in the box, however, you can use formatting attributes such as fonts, bold, center, underline, etc., as well as set tabs. You may practice putting text in a graphics box on your own. You will find it to be quite easy.

▶ GRAPHICS LINES

Horizontal lines are used in documents to set different sections of text apart. Sometimes they simply dress up a document. You can adjust the thickness, the length, and the position of graphics lines as well as how black they are. We'll create four horizontal lines so you get an idea of how to manipulate them. Vertical lines are manipulated in the same way.

1. Press **Alt-F9** and choose **2** Graphics **L**ines. Choose **1** **C**reate to open the Create Graphics Line dialog box. Look at the choices available.

2. Set the thickness at **0.10**. This line will be a tenth of an inch thick. We'll leave all the rest of the defaults for this line. Return to your document screen and look at your line.

3. Create another line that is **0.08** thick. Choose **2** **H**orizontal position and chose Centered. Choose **3** **V**ertical position and set it at **1.5** inches from the top of the page. Choose **5** **L**ength and set it at **5** inches. Return to your document screen and look.

4. Create another centered line that is **0.06** thick, **3.5** inches long, and **2** inches from the top of the page. Return to your document screen and look at your three lines.

5. Create one more centered line that is **0.04** thick, **2.5** inches from the top of the page, and **2** inches long. Are your lines beautiful? Print them and save the document as **lines**. Keep it open.

6. Using your mouse pointer, point to any one of the lines and click once. Sizing handles should appear around the line. Grab the one at the center bottom and drag it down until the line is about a half-inch thick. Point to the line and double click to open the Edit Graphics Line dialog box.

7. Choose **7** **C**olor and then **C**hoose Color. Set the percentage of shading to **25** and return to your document. Are you beginning to get ideas about what you can do with lines?

8. Play with your lines a little more, if you wish. Then close the document without saving.

▶ **EXERCISE 15-4**

Open the **G**raphics menu and choose Graphics **L**ines and **C**reate.

▶ BORDERS

The Borders feature can be used to enclose your pages, paragraphs, or columns. What's more, you can customize the border styles, if you'd like. We'll experiment briefly with Borders.

> **EXERCISE 15-5**
>
> Open the **G**raphics menu. Choose B**o**rders and **P**aragraph.

1. Open **gesthaus**. Press **Alt-F9** to open the Graphics dialog box. Choose **3** B**o**rders and **1** **P**aragraph. Choose OK and return to your document. All four of your paragraphs are enclosed in a border.

2. Look at the document with Print Pre**v**iew. Reveal your codes and delete the [Para Border] code.

3. With your cursor at the beginning of the document, give it a Page border. Look at it in Print Pre**v**iew. Then reveal your codes and delete the border code.

4. Block the first paragraph of **gesthaus**. Give it a Paragraph border.

5. Block the third paragraph and go to the Paragraph Borders dialog box. Choose **1** **B**order Style and Thick Border. Press **Enter** and then **Home, F7** to return to your document. Look at the thick border. The text looks a little crowded.

6. With the cursor still in the third paragraph, return to the Edit Paragraph Border dialog box and choose **3** **C**ustomize. Quite a lot of options are available in this dialog box.

7. Choose **4** **S**pacing. Deselect **1** **A**utomatic Spacing and choose **5** **In**side Spacing. Set left, right, top, and bottom at **0.1** or a tenth of an inch. Return to your document. Does the third paragraph look better?

8. Print the document. Then close it, saving it as **border.1**.

You've experimented with both Page and Paragraph borders. Let's try a short exercise with Column borders.

> **EXERCISE 15-6**
>
> Open the **G**raphics menu. Choose B**o**rders and **C**olumn.

1. Open **columns.1**. Press **Alt-F9**. Choose **3** B**o**rders and then **3** **C**olumn.

2. Choose **1** **B**order Style. We don't want the borders only between columns. We want them all the way around. In the Border Styles dialog box, notice the choices regarding the kinds of borders. Press ↓ and choose Outside and Between.

3. Return to your document screen and check on your Column borders. Use Print Pre**v**iew, if necessary, to see how they really look.

4. Print the document. Then close it, saving it as **border.2**.

Obviously there are quite of number of other things you can do with Borders. You will find as you work with them that they really improve the appearance of some documents.

EQUATIONS

Finally, let's take a look at the WordPerfect Equation Editor. It is great for creating mathematical expressions for engineering, scientific, and business purposes. A graphics box is created for each equation. Most printers can print the characters in equations. They may be printed graphically if the characters aren't part of the font.

▶ **EXERCISE 15-7a**

1. Press **Alt-F9**, choose **1** Graphics **B**oxes and **1** **C**reate.
2. Choose **Y** St**y**le and move the highlight to Equation Box. Press **Enter** and choose **3** Cr**e**ate Equation.
3. Look at the three-part window and identify the parts as you read about them.

Open the **G**raphics menu and choose Graphics **B**oxes and **C**reate.

Find the Button Bar at the top. The large window at the top left is the View Equation window. Below the View window is the Type Equation Text window. This is your work space. Your cursor is there now.

On the right is the equation palette. The Commands pop-up menu at the top contains eight menus, including a variety of symbols, characters, arrows, and others.

▶ **EXERCISE 15-7b**

1. Key the following simple equation: **a + b = c**
2. Redisplay the equation in the display window using one of these four methods:
   - If you have a mouse, click Redisplay on the Button Bar.
   - If you have a mouse, click in the View Equation window.
   - Choose Redisplay from the **V**iew menu.
   - Press **Ctrl-F3**.
3. Your equation will look like Figure 15-8. Despite the fact that you keyed spaces, none appear unless you key tilde characters (~) where you want the spaces.

$a+b=c$

FIGURE 15-8

4. Remove the spaces and replace them with ~ characters. Redisplay the equation. It should look like Figure 15-9.

$a + b = c$

FIGURE 15-9

5. Edit the equation so it looks like this:

   a~+~b over d~=~c

   Space with the **Space Bar** before and after the word **over**. (You could choose that word from the equation palette. It's easier to key it.) Redisplay the equation. It should now look like Figure 15-10.

$a + \dfrac{b}{d} = c$

FIGURE 15-10

6. You can put all of the **a + b** section over **d** by adding curly braces to the equation:

    {a~+~b} over d~=~c

    Do that now and redisplay the equation. It should look like Figure 15-11.

$$\frac{a+b}{d} = c$$

FIGURE 15-11

7. Press **F7** until you return to your document window. The equation is displayed in normal size there. Look at it in Print Pre**v**iew. Return to the document screen and point to the equation with the mouse pointer. Click the left button. Note that the graphics box can be selected, sized, and moved just like the rest of the graphics boxes. Deselect the box.

8. Press **Enter** a couple of times below your equation and read on.

INLINE EQUATIONS

You can also put equations into the line of writing of your text. The procedure is almost the same. Key the text to the point where the equation is to be inserted. Then, instead of choosing Equation in the Box Style dialog box, choose Inline Equation. Create the equation using the Equation Editor in the same way as in the equations in Exercise 7b.

When you return to your document, the equation will be within the text. If the equation is tall, you will need to spread the lines of text to make room for the equation.

1. Key the sentences in Figure 15-12. When you get to the formula, follow the steps below the figure to enter the formula.

▶ **EXERCISE 15-8**

FIGURE 15-12

> The researchers have worked long and hard to find a solution to the problem discussed in your article. It was finally decided that the formula $x^2 + \frac{y^2}{de} = m^2$ is the best solution. That problem is as easy to solve as $\sqrt{144}$.

2. Go to the Create Graphics Box dialog box and choose **Y** for Box Style. Then choose Inline Equation Box and **3** Cr**e**ate Equation.

3. Key the equation as in Exercise 7b, using tildes for the spaces. For the superscripted 2 characters, choose *sup* from the equation palette. You may choose it with the mouse or press **Tab** twice to move the cursor to the palette. The square root symbol in the second sentence is also *sqrt* chosen from the palette.

4. Make your exercise pretty. When you finish, print your equation work. Save your equations in one document named **equation** and close it.

That was a VERY brief introduction to the Equation feature. If you have need of it in your work, you should have no trouble figuring out how to prepare your equations.

▶ MISCELLANEOUS GRAPHICS

With your WordPerfect skills and training you've had in this lesson and your previous lessons, you can do some pretty wonderful things with WordPerfect. You learned earlier about bullets and other characters that dress up your documents.

For example, you can add *dropped caps* to the first letter of the first word of the first line in a document—just like they do in magazine articles. To do this, create a user box that doesn't have any inside or outside border.

You can key text right through your graphics. Some graphics are designed for that precise purpose. For example, some of the borders that come with various WordPerfect products have a place for you to key a message or center the lines for a special certificate. To do this, you simply choose Through Box in the **T**ext Flows Around Graphic section of the Create Graphics Box dialog box.

You can tell WordPerfect you'd like a watermark. Watermarks are put into your documents like a header or a footer. After you've told WordPerfect to create a watermark, you must go to the Graphics Boxes dialog box to choose the graphics image you'd like to use as the watermark. WordPerfect will automatically cause the graphics image to be very lightly shaded so the text can be read—right over the graphics image.

▶ SUMMARY

This lesson has introduced you to quite a number of applications in which you can use the WordPerfect Graphics features. Put together with everything else you've learned in this course, you should be able to create some pretty fantastic-looking documents.

You have been exposed to most of the features of WordPerfect. There are a few others that you'll have to find on your own. The *WordPerfect Reference* and the *WordPerfect Workbook* both contain a wealth of information about the program. In addition, publications like *WordPerfect The Magazine* provide tips to help you use the program more efficiently. Enjoy your work with WordPerfect!

LESSON 15 NOTES:

ACTIVITY

LESSON 15

1. How does the style of a Text box differ from the style of a Table box?

2. Which choice in the Create Graphics Box dialog box gives you the choice of different kinds of boxes to choose from?

3. What choice did you make in the Image Editor to make the fish face in the opposite direction?

4. What is the name of the choice that enables you to make a graphics line "fatter"?

5. When creating a horizontal line, what setting must be made in the Create Horizontal Line dialog box before you can set the length of the line?

6. What is the name of the feature that enables you to enclose a paragraph or a page within a line?

7. When keying the text for an equation, what character is used to tell WordPerfect to put a space in an equation?

8. What is the name of the feature that enables the WordPerfect user to put an equation in the middle of a sentence?

Reference Question. Turn in the *WordPerfect Reference* to the section on Watermarks. How many Watermarks can you put into a document? In the Additional Information near the end of the section, it tells how your printer knows an ordinary image is to be printed as a watermark. What does WordPerfect do? Turn to the graphic images in Appendix G of the *Reference*. Which two images look like they were designed to be watermarks?

Appendix A

Hardware and Software

This appendix contains a variety of information about using WordPerfect on your computer. The appendix is mostly about how WordPerfect interacts with your computer. This section can be studied on an "as needed" basis.

HARDWARE

WordPerfect 6.0 is a large program. In order to run WordPerfect 6.0 for DOS and interim releases, a hard disk system or a networked system is required. Whether on a network or a standalone hard disk system, a lot of hard disk space (approximately 15M for a complete installation and 7M for a partial installation) is required for just the program files.

You may run WordPerfect 6.0 with or without a mouse. As in previous versions of WordPerfect, the function keys may be used to access all features. A function key template is shipped with the software to help the user identify the correct keystroke combinations for nearly 70 WordPerfect features.

In addition, all features are available from the pull-down menus. Whether you access the menus from the keyboard or with a mouse will depend on the user and, of course, the availability of a mouse. Most users will find that some features are more easily accessed with function keystrokes and others are more easily accessed with the mouse and/or pull-down menus. Instructions for using a mouse are included in Appendix B.

INSTALLATION

When WordPerfect 6.0 for DOS is installed, it creates a number of directories. The **WP60** directory contains most of the WordPerfect program files. These include the working files, the help files, a subdirectory containing the graphics files, a subdirectory containing the shipping macros, a subdirectory containing the learning files, and a host of other files that make the program work. The **WP60DOS** directory is a shared files directory. It contains files such as the Speller, Thesaurus, Grammatik, and the printer files. The **WPDOCS** directory contains some prerecorded formats, such as a memo and a newsletter format. It is also the default directory for your documents when you create them.

When installing to the file server of a network, the network supervisor must set up the network software to give the users access and to accommodate changes to the set files for the users. An operating knowledge of the network software, as well as of the setup procedures for WordPerfect, will make the setup of WordPerfect on a network more easily accomplished.

The installation of WordPerfect on your computer is easily accomplished. The procedure is to put the Install 1 disk in the appropriate drive. Then key the drive letter followed by a colon and the word **install** (for example, **a:install** or **b:install**). Press Enter and follow the on-screen prompts.

Because WordPerfect 6.0 installs into the **WP60** directory, it will not affect earlier versions of WordPerfect that you might have running. The **WP60** directory is created on Drive C unless you specify otherwise.

At the beginning of the installation process, WordPerfect checks to see if there is enough room on the hard drive for the program. If a prompt tells you that not enough room exists for all of the WordPerfect files, you may delete unneeded files from your hard disk to make more space available. You may also choose Custom Installation and then Minimum Installation to install only those files necessary for running WordPerfect. This option requires only 7M of free disk space and does not install the Learning Files, Speller, Grammatik, Thesaurus, the preset Button Bars, macros, and graphics. After you install, you may turn to Appendix M of the *WordPerfect Reference* to see what other unneeded files may be deleted.

PRINTERS

WordPerfect 6.0 supports several hundred printers–ranging from dot matrix printers to ink jet printers to high-volume laser printers. In addition to the company-supported printers, a number of user-submitted printer descriptions are available.

WordPerfect is a very printer-dependent program. Even the document appearance on the screen is affected by the printer chosen. While printer descriptions can be changed after a document has been created, it is best to choose the printer before beginning a document. The printer description is saved with each document. This is important to people who are working with several printers. Sometimes it is necessary to open a document before printing in order to send the document to the printer using the correct printer description.

Early in the installation process WordPerfect provides you with an opportunity to choose the printer(s) you will be using. You may install additional printers later. You may also install additional files at any time (like the Speller) by inserting the Install 1 disk and starting the install process as above. Then choose Custom Installation and select the files to be installed.

STARTING WORDPERFECT

Depending on your system configuration, there are a number of ways to start WordPerfect. If you are working on a network, there will be a series of menus to take you into the program. You may need to enter a network access code.

If you are working on a stand-alone hard drive system, you might have a hard drive menu system from which you can choose WordPerfect. Otherwise, on most systems you'll need to go to the **C:\WP60>** prompt and key **wp**. If your WordPerfect 6.0 files are in a different directory, access that directory before attempting to start WordPerfect. During the installation process, WordPerfect checks your **autoexec.bat** file and inserts WP60 into the path statement so you should be able to start WordPerfect from a variety of locations.

CHANGING DRIVES AND DIRECTORIES

Develop the habit of separating your documents saved on disk into directories, just like you separate documents stored on paper in file folders containing related documents. WordPerfect provides features that make it easy to create directories, work within directories, and copy documents between directories. You can create directories within directories and move with ease between the directories on your disk, whether it is a floppy disk or a hard drive.

Terminology. Before working with directories, a few terms need to be defined. The *Root* directory is the first level of files stored on a disk. The *Current* directory is the directory in which you are working at any time. The term *Parent* refers to the directory a level above the directory in which you are working. When your File Manager is showing on the screen, *Current* and *Parent* appear at the top of the list of files. For most purposes, *Directory* and *Subdirectory* are the same thing.

Create a Directory. You may create a directory by opening your File Manager and choosing **H Ch**ange Default Directory. WordPerfect will ask for the name of the directory to which you would like to change. If that directory exists, you will be moved into it. If the directory doesn't exist, WordPerfect will ask if you would like to create it. When you have created a directory, the directory name will appear at the top of the File Manager list followed by the *<Dir>* designation. The directory you are in is the parent to the directory just created.

Moving to a Directory. You can look at the contents of a directory or retrieve a document from a directory using the File Manager. If you are woking with a parent directory and one layer of directories within that parent, open the File Manager and move the highlight to the desired directory. Press Enter. The contents of that directory will be displayed for your use. You have not, however, changed directories. The next time you open the File Manager, the directory that appears will be the original one.

Changing Directories. If you wish to work in a directory other than the parent directory, you can highlight the desired directory and press **H Ch**ange Default Directory. You will need to confirm the change. To return to the parent directory, open the File Manager, highlight *Parent*, press **H Ch**ange Default Directory, and confirm the move.

Changing Drives. If you are working in a directory on the hard drive and wish to work on the disk in Drive A, you may use a similar procedure. From anywhere in the File Manager, press **H Ch**ange Default Directory. In the dialog box that appears, key **a:** and press Enter. WordPerfect will make the disk in Drive A your default directory. The reverse procedure is used to return to the hard drive.

There are other ways of creating and moving between directories. When you begin working with directories, experiment with temporary changes and changes in the defaults. It is much easier than keying the complete filepath and document name each time you wish to retrieve or save a document in a directory other than the root directory.

CHANGING DEFAULTS

WordPerfect comes complete with some settings that might not be right for your business. Many of these settings can be found by accessing the Setup dialog box with Shift-F1. However, not all setup is done from this dialog box. Many of the setup choices must be made from individual dialog boxes related to the feature you are changing. A `Setup . . . Shift+F1` button tells you that setup options are available for that dialog box.

The Screen Setup is available in the **V**iew menu. Printer setup choices are made from the Print Dialog box. The Initial Font can be chosen from the Font dialog box. (Initial Font is the font that is chosen each time you begin a new WordPerfect document.) The Initial Font setting, as well as a number of other Initial Codes, can be set in the Document Format dialog box. If you wanted to make a permanent change to your margins, justification, or line spacing, for example, you could do that in the Initial Codes Setup portion of the Document Format dialog box.

Location of Files, however is still chosen from the Setup dialog box. Press Shift-F1 now and choose **L**ocation of Files. WordPerfect provides a *personal path* and a *shared path* for many of the choices in this dialog box. For example, you can set the personal path for Macros/Keyboards/Button Bar at **a:** if that is where your documents are being stored. If you set the shared path at **C:\WP60\MACROS**, WordPerfect will be able to find the shipping macros as well as your own macros when they are needed. The same is true of the Button Bars.

You may wish to set **7 D**ocuments at **a:** so that your documents are automatically saved to Drive A each time you save them. When you don't insert any setting, your backup files (WordPerfect backs up your work every 10 minutes) are automatically saved as **wp{wpc}.bk?** in the **WP60** directory. The question mark represents the document screen on which you're working. Since you can have as many as nine documents open at one time, the backup files could range from **bk1** to **bk9**.

Appendix B

Using a Mouse

If your computer is equipped with a mouse, there are several ways you can use it in WordPerfect 6.0. While the use of the mouse won't take the place of the keys on the keyboard for all WordPerfect functions, its use can enhance your work with WordPerfect.

HAND POSITION

If you are left-handed, many mouse programs enable you to switch the responses of the mouse buttons so that you can use the mouse with your left hand. Many people who are left handed use the mouse with their right hand with little adjustment because the actions of the fingers with the mouse are new, regardless of which hand you use.

For right-hand use, your thumb should be aligned on the left side of the mouse, and your ring finger and pinkie should be positioned on the right side of the mouse. Your index finger should rest above the left mouse button and your middle finger should rest above the right mouse button.

When you position your hand on the mouse, the mouse should be held with the cord away from you. Your hand and a portion of your forearm should rest comfortably behind the mouse. Most of the movement of the mouse will also involve the movement of your hand and forearm. Try to keep your wrist straight and minimize the action of the wrist in moving the mouse to reduce the chance of repetitive motion injuries to your wrist.

▶ CLICKING

As you move the mouse in your document, a pointer will move on the screen. This pointer is NOT your cursor. One of the more useful functions of the mouse is to position the cursor in a particular place in your document. This may be called "clicking an insertion point" because you point to the desired location for the cursor and click the left mouse button once.

▶ MENUS

The mouse can also be used for accessing the pull-down menus. You do not have to hold the mouse button for the menu to stay open. Then you can use the mouse or the keyboard (keying the *mnemomic*–the bolded or underlined letter) to make your menu selections.

▶ BLOCKING TEXT

One of the most valuable uses of the mouse in WordPerfect is for blocking text. While text can be blocked by positioning the cursor, turning on Block, and moving the cursor to the end of the text to be blocked, it is much easier to use the mouse to drag across the text to be blocked. With a little practice you can become skilled in the exact placement of the mouse pointer at the beginning and the end of the text being blocked. As mentioned in Lesson 6, you can also double-click to block a word, triple-click to block a sentence, or quadruple-click to block a paragraph.

Command Reference

Feature	Function	Menu	Lesson
Begin Outline	Ctrl-T	Tools, Outline	14
Block	Alt-F4 or F12	Edit, Block	6
Block Protect	Shift-F8, O	Layout, Other	12
Bold	Ctrl-B or F6	Font, Appearance	4
Bookmark, Find	Ctrl-F or Shift-F12	Edit, Bookmark	8
Bookmark, Insert	Ctrl-Q or Shift-F12	Edit, Bookmark	8
Borders	Alt-F9, O	Graphics, Borders	15
Button Bar	–	View, Button Bar	8
Bulleted List	Ctrl-F5, O	Tools, Outline	14
Cascade	Ctrl-F3	Window	8
Center	Shift-F6	Layout, Alignment	4
Character Sets	Ctrl-W	Font, WP Characters	4
Close File	– –	File, Close	1
Columns	Alt-F7, C	Layout, Columns	14
Copy	Ctrl-C	Edit, Copy	6
Create Directory	F5, Enter, H	File, File Manager	Appendix A
Create Table	Alt-F7	Layout, Tables	9
Cut	Ctrl-X	Edit	6
Dash (em dash)	Ctrl-W, –	Font, WP Characters	4
Dash Character	Home, Hyphen	Layout, Special Codes	4
Date Code	Shift-F5, C	Tools, Date	5

Feature	Function	Menu	Lesson
Date Text	Shift-F5, T	Tools, Date	5
Delete Line	Ctrl-End	–	2
Delete to Left	Backspace	–	2
Delete to Right	Delete	–	2
Delete Word	Ctrl-Backspace	–	2
Document Initial Fonts	Shift-F8, D	Layout, Document	4
Dot Leaders	Alt-F7, Alt-F7	–	4
Double Indent	Shift-F4	Layout, Alignment	4
Edit Outline	Ctrl-O	Tools, Outline	14
Edit Table	Alt-F11	Layout, Tables	9
ENDFIELD Code	F9	Tools, Merge, Define	10
Endnote	Ctrl-F7, E	Layout, Endnote	12
ENDRECORD Code	Shift-F9, E	Tools, Merge, Define	10
Envelope	Alt-F12	Layout, Envelope	11
Envelopes	Ctrl-F9, Merge	Tools, Merge, Run	11
Equations	Alt-F9, B	Graphics, Graphics Box	15
Exit	F7	File, Exit	1
FIELD Code	Shift-F9, F	Tools, Merge, Define	10
Field Names	Shift-F9, N	Tools, Merge, Define	10
File Manager	F5, Enter	File	3
Flush Right	Alt-F6	Layout, Alignment	4
Fonts	Ctrl-F8, F	Font, Font	4
Footers	Shift-F8, H	Layout, Header/Footer/Watermark	12
Footnote	Ctrl-F7, F	Layout, Footnote	12
Frame Document	Ctrl-F3, W	Window	8

Feature	Function	Menu	Lesson
Go To	Ctrl-Home	Edit, Go To	2
Grammatik	Alt-F1, G	Tools, Writing Tools	7
Graphics Box	Alt-F9, B	Graphics, Graphics Boxes	15
Graphics Lines	Alt-F9, L	Graphics, Graphics Lines	15
Graphics Mode	Ctrl-F3	View	15
Hanging Indent	F4, Shift-Tab	Layout, Alignment	4
Hard Page Break	Ctrl-Enter	Layout, Alignment	2
Hard Space	Home, Space	Layout, Special Codes	4
Headers	Shift-F8, H	Layout, Header/Footer/Watermark	12
Help	F1	Help, Contents	1
Horizontal Line	Alt-F9, L	Graphics, Line	15
Hyphenation	Shift-F8, L	Layout, Line	7
Indent	F4	Layout, Alignment	4
Initial Codes Setup	Shift-F8, D	Layout, Document	4
Inline Equations	Alt-F9, B	Graphics, Graphics Box	15
Italics	Ctrl-I	Font, Appearance	4
Justification	Shift-F8, L	Layout, Justification	15
KEYBOARD Code	Shift-F9, K	Tools, Merge, Define	10
Labels, Create	Shift-F8, P	Layout, Page	11
Left/Right Indent	Shift-F4	Layout, Alignment	4
Left/Right Margins	Shift-F8	Layout, Margins	5
Line Sort	Ctrl-F9, S	Tools, Sort	11

Feature	Function	Menu	Lesson
Line Spacing	Shift-F8	Layout, Line	5
Macro, Edit	Ctrl-F10	Tools, Macro	13
Macro, Play	Alt-F10	Tools, Macro	13
Macro, Record	Ctrl-F10	Tools, Macro	13
Margin Set	Shift-F8	Layout, Margins	5
Merge	Ctrl-F9, M	Tools, Merge, Run	10
Merge Sort	Ctrl-F9, S	Tools, Sort	11
New Page Number	Shift-F8, P	Layout, Page	12
Newspaper Columns	Alt-F7	Layout, Columns	14
Open	F5 or Shift-F10	File	1
Outline	Ctrl-F5, O	Tools, Outline	14
Page Break	Ctrl-Enter	Layout, Alignment	2
Page Mode	Ctrl-F3	View	1, 8
Page Numbering	Shift-F8, P	Layout, Page	12
Page Print	Shift-F7, P	File, Print	3
Paper Size/Type	Shift-F8, P	Layout, Page	9
Paragraph Numbering	Ctrl-F5, O	Tools, Outline	12
Paragraph Sort	Ctrl-F9, S	Tools, Sort	11
Parallel Columns	Alt-F7	Layout, Columns	14
Paste	Ctrl-V	Edit	6
Print	Shift-F7, Enter	File	3
Print Preview	Shift-F7, V	File	3
Printer Control	Shift-F7, C	File, Print	3

Feature	Function	Menu	Lesson
Redline	Ctrl-F8, A	Font, Redline	4
Replace	Alt-F2	Edit	6
Retrieve	Shift-F10	File	1
Reveal Codes	Alt-F3 or F11	View, Reveal Codes	4
Save	Ctrl-F12 or F7	File	1
Save As	F10 or F7	File	1
Search	F2	Edit	6
Select Text	Alt-F5 or F12	Edit	6
Select Records	Ctrl-F9, S	Tools, Sort	11
Setup	Shift-F1	File	13
Soft Page Break	Automatic	–	2
Sort	Ctrl-F9, S	Tools, Sort	11
Spell	Ctrl-F2	Tools, Writing Tools	7
Strikeout	Ctrl-F8, A	Font, Strikeout	4
Suppress	Shift-F8, P	Layout, Page	12
Switch	Shift-F3	Window	8
Switch To	F3	Window	8
Tab	Tab	–	5
Tab Set	Shift-F8, L	Layout, Line or Tab Set	5
Table, Create	Alt-F7, T	Layout, Table	9
Text Columns	Alt-F7, C	Layout, Columns	14
Text Mode	Ctrl-F3	View	8
Thesaurus	Alt-F1	Tools, Writing Tools	7
Tile Documents	Ctrl-F3	Window	8
Undelete	Escape	Edit, Undelete	2
Underline	Ctrl-U or F8	Font, Appearance	4

Feature	Function	Menu	Lesson
Undo	Ctrl-Z	Edit, Undo	2
Vertical Line	Alt-F9, L	Graphics, Line	15
Watermark	Shift-F8, H	Layout, Header/Footer/Watermark	15
Widow/Orphan	Shift-F8, O	Layout, Other	12
Windowing	Ctrl-F3	Window	8
Zoom	Ctrl-F3	View	8

MOVING THE CURSOR

End	End of the line
Home, Home, ←	Beginning of the line
Home, Home, ↑	Top of the document (below codes first character)
Home, Home, Home, ↑	Top of the document (above all codes)
Home, Home, ↓	Bottom of the document
Page Up	Top of previous page
Page Down	Top of next page
Keypad Minus Key (-) or Home, ↑	Top of screen
Keypad Plus Key (+) or Home, ↓	Bottom of screen
Ctrl →	Beginning of next word
Ctrl ←	Beginning of previous word
Ctrl-Home, →	To the column at the right
Ctrl-Home, ←	To the column at the left
Ctrl-Home, Ctrl-Home	Returns cursor to last position

DELETING TEXT

Backspace	Deletes character to the left of the cursor
Delete	Deletes character at the cursor
Ctrl-Delete	Deletes word at the cursor
Ctrl-Backspace	Deletes word at the cursor
Ctrl-End	Deletes from the cursor to the end of the line
Ctrl-Page Down	Deletes from the cursor to the end of the page

Index

A

adding text, 11
Auto Code Placement, 39

B

Backspace key, 11
begin a new page, 13
Block Protect, 120
blocked text
    copying and moving, 53
    deleting, 52
    formatting, 51
blocking text, 50
    from the keyboard, 50
    using a mouse, 51
blocks
    printing, 55
    saving, 55
Bookmark tool, 73
borders, 148
    page, 149
    paragraph, 149
Box Style dialog box
    Equation, 151
    Inline Equation, 151
bulk mailing, 107
    zip code sort, 107
Button Bar, 21, 70
    default, 71
    setup, 71

C

Caps Lock key, 26
Cascade, 69
changing drives and directories, 159
character formatting, 26
character sets, 29
column, 149
    blocking, 54
    borders, 149
    moving, 54

columns
    balanced, 134
    Balanced Newspaper Columns (Alt-F7), 134
    beginning position, 135
    multiple, 134
    Parallel Columns, 136
        uses, 136
    Text Columns dialog box
        Custom Widths, 135
Command Reference, 165
Conditional End of Page, 120
correcting text
    Backspace key, 11
Create Graphics Line dialog box, 148
creating a data file, 91
creating a form file, 89
Ctrl-Backspace, 12
Ctrl-End, 12
Ctrl-Home
    Go to function, 10
Ctrl-Page Down, 12
cursor, 2
    moving, 10
    moving with mouse, 10
    position in document, 4

D

data file
    table, 94
Data File Options dialog box, 103
data files with named fields, 92
default preferences, 46
defaults
    Button Bar, 71
    changing, 46, 161
Delete key, 11
deleting text, 171
    blocked text, 52
    Delete key, 11
document
    changing the name of, 7
    Filename prompt, 6
    justification, 45
    opening, 6

position in, 3
    Ln indicator, 3
    Pg indicator, 3
resaving, 7
retrieving, 6
Status Line, 3
Document Format dialog box, 105
Document Initial Codes
    Cntr Pgs On, 106
    Labels Form, 106
    Paper Sz/Typ, 106
drive designation, 4
dropped caps, 152

E

Edit Graphics Box dialog box, 146
    Image Editor, 146
Edit Sort Keys Dialog Box, 108
editing
    outlines, 138
endnotes, 118
    Endnote Placement code, 119
envelope
    POSTNET Bar Code, 102
Envelope dialog box, 102
envelopes
    merged, 102
    merging, 102
    POSTNET Bar Code, 103
    printing, 102
    single, 102
equations
    Equation Editor, 150
    inline, 151
    Type Equation Text window, 150
Esc key, 40

F

file management, 22
File Manager, 6, 22
    file size, 22
    printing, 21
    sort files, 22
File menu, 2, 5
    Close, 5
    Exit, 5
    Save, 5
    Save As, 5
file size, 22
Filename prompt, 6

Font dialog box, 27, 28
    Appearance, 28
    Font, 28
    Position, 28
    Relative Size, 28
fonts, 27
    character sets, 29
    proportional, 28
    sizes, 29
    Type 1, 28
footers
    in Page mode, 2
footers See also headers and footers
footnotes, 118
    creating (Ctrl-F7), 118
    in Page mode, 2
footnotes and endnotes
    deleting, 119
    editing, 120
    entering, 119
    viewing in Print Preview, Page mode, 119
form and data files
    merging, 92
form file
    FIELD codes, 89
Format dialog box, 116
    headers and footers, 116
formatting
    blocked text, 51
    Bold, 26
    Caps, 26
    character, 26
    fonts, 27
    Italics, 27
    Redline, 27
    Strikeout, 27
    tables, 79
    Underline, 26
    word, 26
function keys, 165

G

Go to function, 10
grammar checker, 64
Grammatik, 64
graphic boxes
    attach to page, paragraph, character, 147
    button box, 145
    creating, 145
    editing, 146
    figure box, 144

table box, 144
text box, 144
user box, 144
watermarks, 144
graphics
    borders, 148
    Create Graphics Line dialog box, 148
    dropped caps, 152
    lines, 148
    miscellaneous, 152
    sizing handles, 147
    watermark, 152
    watermarks, 144
Graphics dialog box, 145
Graphics mode, 2

H

hardware
    printers, 159
    requirements, 157
Header or Footer dialog box, 117
Header/Footer screen, 117
Header/Footer/Watermark, 116
Header/Footer/Watermark dialog box, 119
headers
    in Page mode, 2
headers and footers, 116
    Auto Code Placement, 117
    editing, 117
    even/odd pages, 116
    Reveal Codes, 117
Home key, 10
hyphenation, 64

I

Image Editor, 146
importing spreadsheets, 85
inline equations, 151
insert mode, 12
inserting text, 12
installation, 158

J

joining tables, 85
Justification, types of, 45

K

keyboard merge, 95
keying and editing text
    screen mode, 2
keying text, 4

L

Labels, 105
landscape orientation, 85
Layout menu, 116
    footnotes and endnotes, 118
    Header/Footer/Watermark, 116
Layout Menus
    headers and footers, 116
Line Format menu, 44
    Justification types, 45
Line Sort, 109
Line Spacing, 44
    paragraph, 44
list, generate with Mark Text, 121

M

macros, 128
    .wpm etension, 129
    Alt macro, 129
    chain and nested, 131
    create and play, 128
    creating (Ctrl-F10), 129
    editing, 129
    list, 131
    named macros, 128
    sample text, 130
    stored location, 129
Macros/Keyboards/Button Bar dialog box, 72
margins
    default, 43
    setting, 43
    side margins, 43
    top and bottom, 44
Mark Text, 121
menu, 2
menu bar, 2
merge
    codes, 88
    data file
        table data file, 88
        text data file, 88
    field, 88
    form file, 88
        creating, 89
    keyboard, 95
    numbered fields, 92
    record, 88
    terminology, 88
Merge Codes Dialog Box, 89
Merge Codes dialog box, 106
merging form and data files, 92
minimize/maximize buttons, 69

mouse
    blocking text, 164
    clicking, 164
    hand position, 163
    pull-down menus, 164
moving a column, 54
moving the cursor, 10, 170
    with a mouse, 10
    with the keyboard, 10
multiple columns, 134

N

newspaper columns, 134
numbered fields, 92

O

opening a document, 6
orientation
    changing, 85, 86
outline
    collapsing, 139
    editing, 138
    options, 138
Outline dialog box, 137
Outline Editor (Ctrl-o), 139
outlining, 136

P

Page, 10
page
    beginning a new, 13
    borders, 149
    changing orientation, 86
    numbering, 117
    orientation, 85
Page Down, 10
page end control
    Block Protect, 120
    Conditional End of Page, 120
    Widow/Orphan Protect, 120
page end controls, 120
    widows and orphans, 120
Page Format dialog box
    Page Numbering, 117, 119
    Suppress, 118
page formatting codes
    suppress, 118
Page mode, 2
Page Numbering, 117
Page Up, 10
paginating text, 13

Paper Size/Type dialog box, 86
paragraph
    borders
        borders, 149
    Line Spacing, 44
paragraph format
    center, 31
    flush right, 31
paragraph formatting, 31
    dot leaders, 32
    hanging indent, 33
    indent, 33
paragraph numbering outline (Ctrl-t), 136
Parallel Columns, 136
portrait orientation, 85
preferences, changing, 46
Print Preview, 21
    Button Bar, 21
    Seeing Header/Footer, 116
Print/Fax dialog box, 20
printer selection, 20
printers, 159
printing, 20
    Document on Disk, 20
    from the File Manager, 21
    from the working screen, 20
    Multiple Pages, 20
    Page, 20
    Print Preview, 21
    printer selection, 20

Q

Quickmark tool, 73

R

Record Macro dialog box, 128
Replace, 56
requirements
    hardware, 157
resaving a document, 7
retrieving a document, 6
Reveal Codes, 34
    open codes, 34
    paired codes, 34
Ribbon, 70
Ribbon tool, 70
Run Merge dialog box, 102
    Blank Fields, 104
    Data Record Selection, 104
    Output, 103
    Page Breaks, 104
    Repeat Merge, 104

S

save, 3
    drive designation, 4
Save dialog box, 3
saving text, 5
Screen Modes, 2
    Graphics mode, 2
screen modes
    Page mode, 2
    Text mode, 2
        keying and editing text, 2
Search, 55
Select, 110
Sort
    Line Sort, 110
sort, 107
    alphabetized, 109
    compound names, 109
    files, 22
    hard spaces, 109
    line, 109
    Paragraph Sort, 110
    Select, 110
    zip code, 108
Sort dialog box, 109
Specify File Manager List dialog box, 5
spell checking, 62
Speller, 62
starting WordPerfect, 159
Status Line, 3
    file name, 3
    filepath, 3
    font, 3
Suppress code, 118
synonym
    finding with the Thesaurus, 63

T

Tab Set Dialog Box, 40
table
    Cell Format, 81
    converting text, 84
    creating a, 78
    editing, 79
    fill and line format, 81
    Floating Cell, 83
    formatting, 79
    formulas, 82
    importing spreadsheets, 85
    joining, 85
    recalculate values, 82
    references to text, 83
    spreadsheet capabilities, 81
    terminology, 78
    vs. tabs, 79
table data file, 88, 94
Table Data File Record, 94
table editor, 79
Table of Contents
    Mark Text, 121
tabs
    adding dot leaders, 42
    moving, 43
    setting, 40
    types of, 42
    vs. tables, 79
text
    adding, 11
    blocked
        copying and moving, 53
        deleting, 52
    blocking, 50
        using a mouse, 51
    bullets, 30
    columns, 134
    converting to table, 84
    correcting, 11
    dash character, 30
    deleting, 11
    formatting
        Bold, 26
        Caps, 26
        fonts, 27
        Italics, 27
        Redline, 27
        Strikeout, 27
        Underline, 26
    formatting after keying, 29
    fractions, 30
    hard space, 30
    hyphenation, 64
    inserting, 12
    keying, 4
    paginating, 13
    references to table, 83
    saving, 5
    smart quotations, 30
    special characters, 30
    tabs, 40
    undelete, 40
text blocking, 50
Text Columns dialog box, 135
text data file, 88, 91
Text mode, 2
Thesaurus, 63

tools
    Bookmark, 73
    Button Bar, 70
    Quickmark, 73
    Ribbon, 70
    writing, 61
Type Equation Text window, 150
Typeover, 12

U

Undelete, 52
Undelete dialog box, 52
Undo, 53
    vs. Undelete, 53
undo command, 40
using a mouse, 163

V

View menu
    Button Bar setup, 71
    Reveal Codes, 34
viewing documents, 68

W

watermark, 152
Widow/Orphan Protect, 120
widows and orphans, 120
Window menu, 69
windowing, 68
    Cascade, 69
    minimize/maximize buttons, 69
word formatting, 26
WordPerfect 6.0 installation, 158
writing tools, 61

Z

zoom, 68
Zoom Menu, 68

WordPerfect 6.1 for DOS UPDATE

Basically, Version 6.1 of WordPerfect for DOS is the same as the 6.0 version. Most of the menus are exactly the same. The choices made with function keys are the same. The choices from the menus and dialog boxes do the same things.

In the following short list, textbook page numbers are listed where differences between the programs are worth noting. If you are using WordPerfect 6.1 for DOS, go through your text now and put a special "6.1" mark on the pages listed below. Then when you come to one of the specially marked pages, return to this update to see what's different in Version 6.1.

When you finish the 15 lessons in the text, turn to the *Special Features* lesson of this Update for practice with some of the new features that were added to the program in the 6.1 version.

- **Page 4**. When keying text in Version 6.1, you will find that WordPerfect corrects some of your errors and changes capitalization as you go. Don't be surprised if this happens. You'll learn more about this feature called QuickCorrect in the *Special Features* lesson.
- **Page 6**. The arrangement of the features in the Version 6.1 File Manager dialog box is slightly different.
- **Page 22**. Again, look at the File Manager dialog box in Version 6.1. Sort By has been removed from the list of features at the right and is combined with Setup on a Sort/Setup button at the bottom of the dialog box. This feature may be accessed by pressing Shift-F1 or clicking the Sort/Setup button. Also in this dialog box, you can create a new directory if you choose **9**.
- **Page 40**. In Version 6.1 you can set your tabs and margins using a mouse and the Ruler. Choose Ruler from the View menu to display the bar. Drag the existing tabs (the black triangles) from place to place or off the Ruler completely. Click in the desired location on the Ruler to set a new tab. Select different tab types by pointing on the Ruler and clicking the right mouse button. Then click the new tab stops into place. An exercise using the Ruler is included in the *Special Features* lesson.
- **Page 72**. When setting the preferences for macros, use **WP61** instead of **WP60** for the filepath of the directory containing the macros.

- **Pages 82 and 84**. Version 6.1 contains a Table menu. Use this for creating and formatting tables instead of choosing Tables from the Layout menu.
- **Page 129**. Version 6.1 macros are stored in the **C:\wp61\macros** directory.
- **Page 145**. The graphics image used in this lesson comes with the Version 6.0 software but not the Version 6.1 software. For that reason, the image may be included on the template disk. If you can't find **fishtrop.wpg**, use the **rose.wpg** graphics image for the exercises beginning with Exercise 15-1. It is in the **c:\wp61\graphics** directory. Adjust the exercises as necessary to accommodate this substitution. WordPerfect 6.1 for DOS has 55 graphics images, many of which are borders and "enders."
- **Appendix A**. The WordPerfect 6.1 for DOS directories are **WP61, WPC61DOS**, and **WPDOCS**. Adjust the instructions accordingly.

◆ WordPerfect 6.1 for DOS SPECIAL FEATURES

OBJECTIVES

Upon completion of this lesson, you will be able to:

1. Use QuickMenus to choose WordPerfect features.
2. Correct your errors with the QuickCorrect feature.
3. Format document parts with QuickFormat.
4. Use the Drop Caps feature.
5. Adjust the document size with the Make It Fit feature.
6. Set tabs and margins with the Ruler.
7. Use WordPerfect Templates.
8. Discuss locating documents with document histories.

Estimated Time: 1 hour

If you are using Version 6.1, a number of features have been added to the program to enhance its use. These features include QuickMenus, QuickCorrect, and QuickFormat, as well as a number of less obvious features that make the program run faster and make it easier to use.

In this update lesson, you will learn the most useful of the new WordPerfect features. As with the other features you have learned, only a brief introduction to each feature is provided. You will want to explore the features more on your own when you finish your training. Proceed through the exercises in this lesson if you are using Version 6.1. If you are working with WordPerfect 6.0, you may read to see what you are missing, or you may skip it. Your instructor will give you specific instructions regarding this lesson.

QUICKMENUS

If you use a mouse with WordPerfect, a series of QuickMenus put feature selection readily at your fingertips. The content of each of the QuickMenus is determined by the location of the mouse pointer when you click the right mouse button. There are quite a number of QuickMenus. Let's experiment.

6.1 Update: Exercise 1

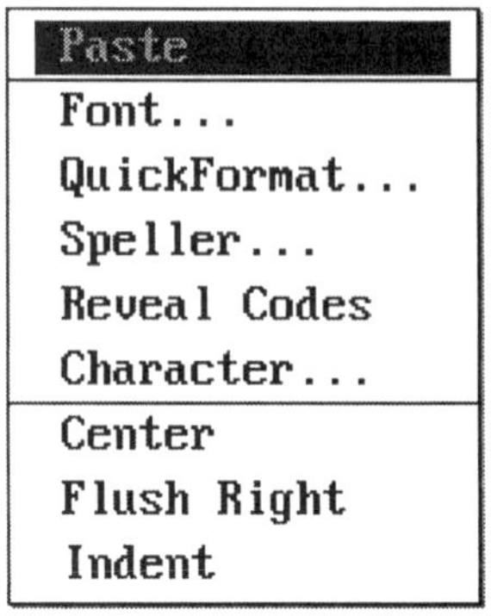

1. Open **columns.1**. Point to any location in the text and click the right mouse button.

2. Look at the choices in the QuickMenu that appears. Center, Flush Right, Reveal Codes, and a number of others are included. The QuickMenu should look much like Figure 1.

3. Point to the left margin and right click. Look at the choices available now.

```
Paste
Font...
QuickFormat...
Speller...
Reveal Codes
Character...
Center
Flush Right
Indent
```
Figure 1

4. Change to Page mode. Point to the top margin and right click. Now you can choose Headers, Footers, etc.

5. Close **columns.1** and open **sales.6**.

6. Point to the table and right click. Notice that most of the features needed for formatting tables appear in this QuickMenu.

7. Close **sales.6** without saving.

In addition to being able to choose formatting features for the tables using QuickMenu, you should note that in WordPerfect 6.1 you can actually format tables without having to go to the table editor. When you learned to work with tables in Lesson 9, you used the table editor for everything except entering text into your tables. In WordPerfect 6.0, using the table editor is the only way to format tables.

QUICKCORRECT

The QuickCorrect feature corrects specified keying errors. You may have noticed that the first letter of a word following a period is automatically capitalized. So is the first word of a document. QuickCorrect fixes your error when you accidentally capitalize the first two letters of a word. It also fixes more than 100 commonly misspelled words. Let's see what QuickCorrect does with this simple exercise.

6.1 Update: Exercise 2

1. Memorize the sentence in Figure 2, complete with errors.

2. Watch your screen as you key the sentence so you can see the corrections as they are made. When you finish, close your practice document without saving it.

```
THe dog adn cat are in teh barn.
```
Figure 2

Did you notice that the corrections in the misspelled words took place when you pressed the space bar following the word? Words and phrases can be added to QuickCorrect to help you work faster. For example, you can tell QuickCorrect to replace **wp** with *WordPerfect 6.1 for DOS*. You must go to the QuickCorrect dialog box to do this. QuickCorrect is one of the Writing Tools chosen from the Layout menu. So that you can see how it works, let's add an entry in the QuickCorrect list. Then we'll remove it again.

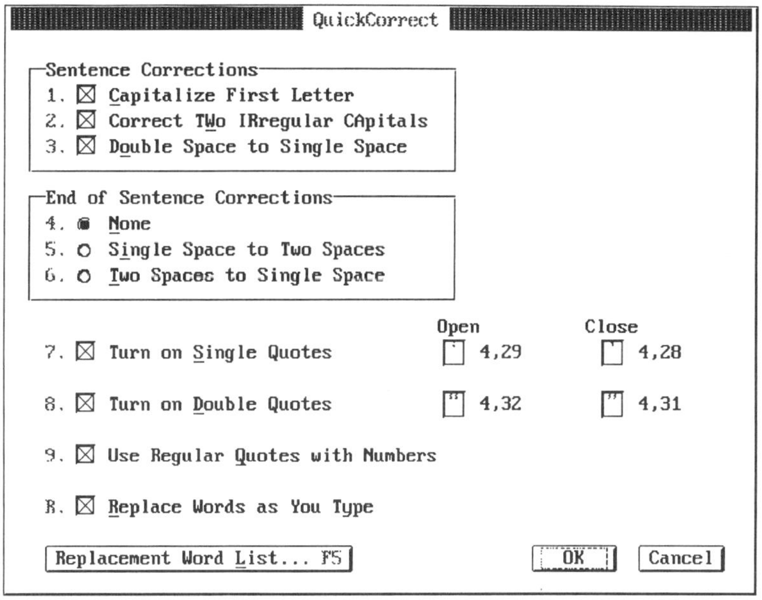

Figure 3

6.1 Update: Exercise 3

1. Choose **Q**uickCorrect from the **W**riting Tools menu. Look at Figure 3. It contains options for corrections to be made as you key your documents.

2. Press **F5** to display the list of replacement words that come with the program. Scroll through the list and look at some of the entries.

3. Choose **1 A**dd Entry and key **bbc** in the Word box. Tab once. In the Replacement box, key **Butte des Morts Business College**. Click OK.

4. Close the dialog box and click OK to return to your document.

5. Key **bbc** and space once. Does this look kind of like the macro you created for the Werneck Gesthaus Posthotel?

6. Return to the QuickCorrect word list (from the Layout menu). Scroll through the list until your highlight is on the **bbc** entry.

7. Choose **3 D**elete Entry and confirm the deletion. Then return to your document window. Close the document without saving it.

As you can see, it is easy to add words to the list or delete them when you no longer need them. In this case, you deleted the entry so the next class can complete Exercise 3. If you are in a classroom situation, don't make any additional changes to the QuickCorrect list unless your instructor gives you permission to do so.

QUICKFORMAT

QuickFormat may be used to copy formatting such as fonts and attributes from one portion of a document to other portions. What's more, document parts formatted using QuickFormat are linked together so that if you change the formatting of one part, they will all be changed.

In order to practice this feature, we'll begin by adding side headings to one of your earlier documents.

6.1 Update: Exercise 4

1. Open **deskpub.for**. Position the insertion point at the end of the first paragraph and press **Enter** once to add a blank line.

2. Key **Description of Desktop Publishing** as the side heading for the paragraph. (Be sure the side heading has a blank line above it and below it.)

3. Use the same procedure to add the following side headings at the beginning of the next two paragraphs:
   Paragraph 3:   **Printing**
   Paragraph 4:   **Justification for Desktop Publishing**

4. Block one of the side headings. Open the F**o**nt dialog box and choose **B**old, **U**nderline, and Italics. Close the dialog box.

5. With the cursor still in the side heading, right click and choose QuickFormat from the QuickMenu. Be sure the "Automatic Update" box contains an X. Click OK.

6. If you have a mouse, note that the pointer looks like a paint roller (unless you are in Text mode), as illustrated in Figure 4. Look at the red line across the bottom of the window containing instructions.

Figure 4

7. Follow those instructions to apply the format to the other two side headings. Press **Esc** to turn QuickFormat off.

8. With the insertion point in one of the side headings, return to the Font dialog box and turn off Underline. Choose Small **C**aps. Return to your document and check the other side headings.

9. Experiment with QuickFormat. Then keep the practice document open for the next exercise.

QuickFormat can be used to format individual words, items in a list, or whole paragraphs. One of the greatest benefits comes from the fact that if you change your mind, you don't have to change each occurrence of the format individually.

DROP CAPS

Near the end of Lesson 15, WordPerfect 6.0 users are told how to create drop caps at the beginning of their newspaper, newsletter, and magazine articles. Version 6.1 contains a Drop Cap feature that does the job for you. Let's try it.

6.1 Update: Exercise 5

Figure 5

1. Move your cursor to the beginning of the first line of the first paragraph. Delete the Tab that indents the paragraph.

2. Choose Dro**p** Cap from the bottom of the **F**ont menu. In the Drop Cap dialog box, choose **E**dit.

3. The Edit Drop Cap Definition dialog box should appear, looking much like Figure 5.

4. Look at the choices. Then choose OK to return to your document.

5. Experiment with drop cap options, if you wish. Then close the document without saving it.

MAKE IT FIT

Have you ever keyed what was supposed to be a one-page document and ended up with a couple of lines that extended onto the second page? Most of us have. You know WordPerfect well enough so you can experiment with margins, font sizes, line spacing, etc., to make the document fit on one page, but it takes time to fuss with it.

The Make It Fit feature will do that for you, assuming the request is reasonable. The default is to adjust line spacing and font size, although other adjustments may be made with your permission. Let's practice.

6.1 Update: Exercise 6

1. Open **deskpub** from the template disk. (If you don't have the template disk, you may remove all formatting and footnotes from **deskpub.for** for this exercise. Remove the title and all spacing at the top of the document, too.)

2. Be sure Courier 10 is the document font so your exercise will work as designed.

3. Position the cursor at the beginning of the first paragraph. Change to double spacing. Check the length of the document. It should be a little more than 1 page.

4. Choose **Make It Fit** from the middle of the **Layout** menu. The Make It Fit dialog box will look like Figure 6.

5. Tell WordPerfect to make the document fit on 1 page. Be sure that line spacing and font size are the only items selected to be adjusted.

6. Click the Make It Fit button and check your document. Is it on one page? What is the current font size? What is the current line spacing?

7. Close the document without saving.

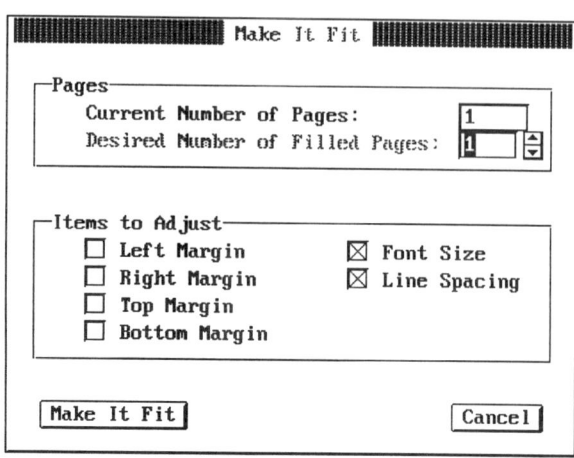

Figure 6

RULER

Available only in Version 6.1 is a Ruler that may be used for setting tabs and margins. This Ruler is chosen from the View menu but can only be used with a mouse. If you have a mouse, let's experiment with margins and tabs using the Ruler. (Note: The Ruler doesn't appear in Text mode.)

6.1 Update: Exercise 7

1. Choose **Ruler** from the **View** menu. Look at the Ruler. The triangles below the Ruler are left tabs. The white space at the top is the margins.

2. Point to the heavy black bar at the left of the margin row and drag it to 2" on the scale. (You have just changed your left margin to 2"). Drag it back to 1".

3. Point to the tab triangle at 3". Drag the triangle down and off the Ruler. You have just removed the tab stop at 3".

4. Point to the place at 3" where you just removed the tab. Click once to replace that tab.

5. Point to any of the tab triangles and click the RIGHT mouse button. Look at the pop-up menu that allows you to choose different tab types.

6. Choose **Clear All Tabs**. Now look at your Ruler.

7. Point in the area where the tabs used to be and right-click again to open the pop-up menu. Choose a **Center** tab and click at 4" on the Ruler to set the tab.

8. Drag the Center tab off the Ruler. For practice, set tabs for the sample in Figure 13-12 on page 165. (You don't need to key the exercise.)

9. Display the pop-up menu and choose **Hide Ruler Bar** to deselect the Ruler. Then close your document without saving.

The Ruler is easy to use. If you are using WordPerfect 6.1 for DOS, you will probably use it for most of your changes to margins and tab stops.

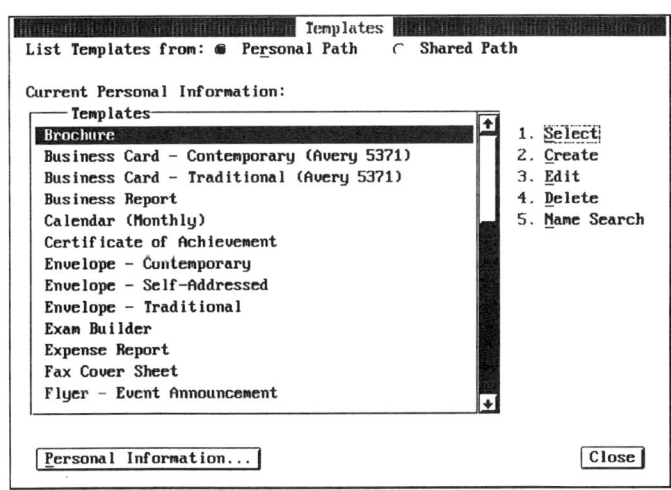

Figure 7

TEMPLATES

More than 30 templates or preformatted documents are included in Version 6.1 when it is shipped. These templates are designed to make it easier to prepare certain kinds of documents. What's more, you can create your own customized templates that can be saved and used repeatedly for your work. Let's look at one of the shipping templates.

6.1 Update: Exercise 8

1. Choose Template from the File menu. A large dialog box should open that looks much like Figure 7.

2. Look through the list. Then choose the Fax Cover Sheet template.

3. Close the Personal Information Sets dialog box.

4. Fill in the boxes of the Template Entries dialog box, as if you were sending the fax to someone you know in a local business. If you do not know the fax and telephone numbers, you may make them up. The fax will be only one page long.

5. When you finish, you will be taken to the document screen, and you may make up a short message.

6. Study the layout of the cover sheet. Think how much time was saved in setup, even though you know enough about WordPerfect to prepare the same document by yourself.

7. Close the document without saving it.

NOTE: You probably know that WordPerfect makes it possible for you to send that fax directly from the print dialog box, providing you have the appropriate communications software and hardware.

You may want to experiment with other templates. Personal information is requested for some of them. If you are

WordPerfect 6.1 for DOS Update to *WordPerfect 6.0 DOS: Quick Course* **U9**

on a classroom computer, your instructor will most likely prefer that you NOT enter personal information because the computer remembers that information for the next template.

HISTORIES

One other feature deserves mention. You may have noticed that a down arrow appears beside the Filename box when you are opening documents. If you click that arrow, WordPerfect will list the last ten documents with which you have worked. This feature saves you the process of scrolling through many documents to find one you recently saved. You may explore this feature on your own.

SUMMARY

As you can see, many useful features have been added to the 6.1 version of WordPerfect for DOS. These features have been only briefly introduced in this lesson. On your own time, explore these features thoroughly. If you remember to use them, they will save much time in your work.

6.1 UPDATE NOTES:

6.1 UPDATE REVIEW ACTIVITY

1. What computer tool must you have to display a QuickMenu? How do you display a QuickMenu?

2. When you misspell a word that is corrected with QuickCorrect, when is the correction made?

3. Why shouldn't you change QuickCorrect if you work in a classroom?

4. What is the advantage of formatting pieces of text with QuickFormat?

5. What two changes appear on your document screen when you have QuickFormat chosen?

6. Do you think WordPerfect would be able to change a document that's nearly two pages long into a one-page document with the Make It Fit tool?

7. Which of the new Version 6.1 features do you like the best? Why?

Reference Question: Several new commands have been added to the list of WordPerfect macro commands. Look in the *WordPerfect 6.1 for DOS Upgrade Guide* for the section on Macro Commands. Which of the new features learned in this lesson are included in the new macro commands?

JOIN US ON THE INTERNET

WWW: http://www.thomson.com
E-MAIL: findit@kiosk.thomson.com

South-Western Educational Publishing is a partner in *thomson.com*, an on-line portal for the products, services, and resources available from International Thomson Publishing (ITP). Through our site, users can search catalogs, examine subject-specific resource centers, and subscribe to electronic discussion lists.

South-Western Educational Publishing is also a reseller of commercial software products. See our printed catalog or view this page at:
http://www.swpco.com/swpco/comp_ed/com_sft.html

For information on our products visit our World Wide Web site at:
http://www.swpco.com/swpco.html

To join the South-Western Computer Education discussion list, send an e-mail message to: **majordomo@list.thomson.com**. Leave the subject field blank, and in the body of your message key: SUBSCRIBE SOUTH-WESTERN-COMPUTER-EDUCATION <your e-mail address>.

A service of I(T)P®

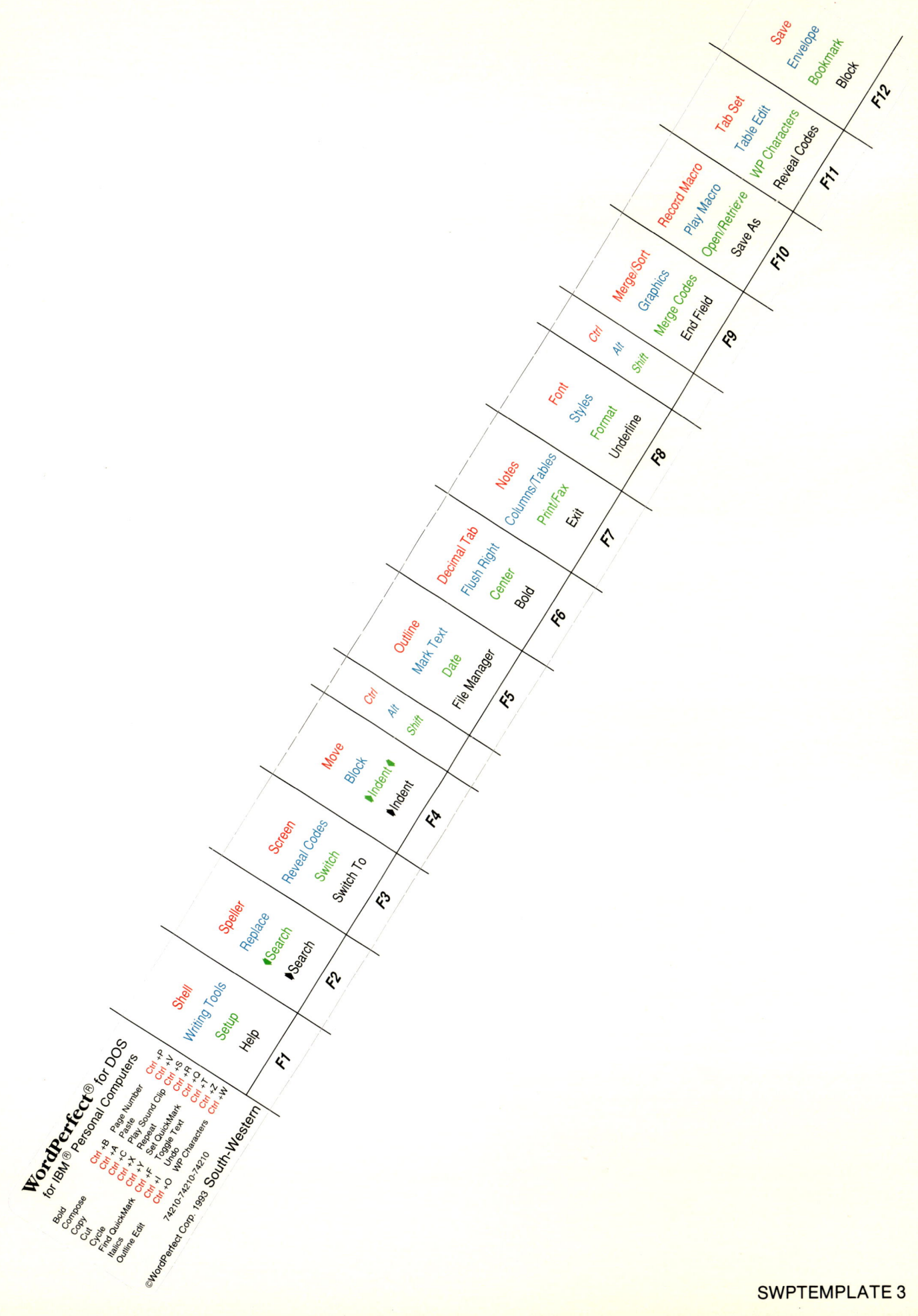

WordPerfect® for DOS
for IBM® Personal Computers

Bold	Ctrl +B	Page Number Ctrl +P
Compose	Ctrl +A	Paste Ctrl +V
Copy	Ctrl +C	Play Sound Clip Ctrl +S
Cut	Ctrl +X	Repeat Ctrl +R
Cycle	Ctrl +Y	Set QuickMark Ctrl +Q
Find QuickMark	Ctrl +F	Toggle Text Ctrl +T
Italics	Ctrl +I	Undo Ctrl +Z
Outline Edit	Ctrl +O	WP Characters Ctrl +W

74210-74210-74210

©WordPerfect Corp. 1993 **South-Western**

F1
- Shell
- Writing Tools
- Setup
- Help

F2
- Speller
- Replace
- ◆Search
- ◆Search

F3
- Screen
- Reveal Codes
- Switch
- Switch To

F4
- Move
- Block
- ◆Indent◆
- ◆Indent

F5
- Ctrl
- Alt
- Shift
- File Manager

F6
- Outline
- Mark Text
- Date
- Bold

F7
- Decimal Tab
- Flush Right
- Center
- Exit

F8
- Notes
- Columns/Tables
- Print/Fax
- Underline

F9
- Ctrl
- Alt
- Shift
- End Field

F10
- Merge/Sort
- Graphics
- Merge Codes
- Save As

F11
- Record Macro
- Play Macro
- Open/Retrieve
- Reveal Codes

F12
- Tab Set
- Table Edit
- WP Characters
- Block

- Save
- Envelope
- Bookmark

SWPTEMPLATE 3